THE ECONOMIC MISSION

JIM WEBER

About the Author

Jim Weber is the founder of Weber Advertising & Marketing, Inc., a mid-size advertising agency which has been successfully operating in Lancaster, PA since 1996. During that time, he and his wife Jennifer, also manage The Cookie Sale to Combat World Hunger which annually provides millions of meals for school-aged children in some of the world's poorest countries. While providing food was good, Jim learned that providing opportunity and eliminating poverty was even better so he created the Economic Mission model. This led him to team with the Sisters of St. Joseph of the Apparition in Praville, Haiti and build a textile factory to provide jobs and opportunity. Price and quality remained high allowing the factory to compete in the global marketplace. As the number of employees grew, both Jim and the Sisters were pleasantly surprised by the improvement in the local economy and the quality of life for the community. Jim now wants to export his Economic Mission concept to other impoverished communities where opportunity will make a difference.

Now… really about Jim Weber.

As a cradle Catholic, Jim was an altar boy, Boy Scout and a mediocre athlete. As a kid, Jim was afraid of failure and was even more afraid of the demands that success would bring. That changed when he learned he could sell and he was pretty good at that. In college, Jim stopped attending Mass, started smoking weed and developed a passion for following the Grateful Dead. Jim has fully participated in all of the 7 deadly sins and has maybe even created other deadly sins along the way. After getting dumped by his girlfriend in the late 80s, he decided to change his life for the better. During this time, his mom was praying fervently for his conversion. Jim met Jennifer who helped him along the way and they married on the same day Go for Gin won the Kentucky Derby. The best part of leaving Catholicism was returning to the faith as a Committed Catholic. By leaning on the Eucharist and Divine Mercy, Jim wants to become a better version of himself each and every day. Jim sees conversion as a verb instead of a noun and strives to make continuous progress. Today, Jim studies philosophy and draws inspiration from the Bible, Buddha and Stoic philosophers like Marcus Aurelius as well as contemporary thinkers like Mother Teresa, Francis Chan and Thomas Sowell. Jim prioritizes values and virtue over blind legalistic adherence. Jim is far from perfect and he is not concerned about being politically correct. Doing the will of God is important to Jim and that is why he is so committed to combating poverty for the poorest of the poor. Although Jim still listens to the Grateful Dead, he stopped the weed habit in the 80s.

Dedication

This book is dedicated to Jennifer, my dear wife, in honor of her continued commitment to helping the poorest of the poor. Her strength and perseverance is as attractive to me as her smile.

This book is also dedicated to the employees of the factory in Praville, Haiti; especially those who went through the original training process in Port-au-Prince, and all who helped prove that the Economic Mission business model can work and to the dedication, wisdom and virtue of Exode Charles.

This book is also dedicated to my small group that meets every Sunday at 9 AM. For over 15 years, my small group has helped me grow as a Christian. It all started as a cookie sale over 25 years ago and my Parish family at Saint Joseph Church in Lancaster, PA turned that into a machine that provides millions of meals for starving people.

This book is also dedicated to the Staff and Clients of Weber Advertising. I've always been supported by these folks in so many ways. It was always personal and it was never just about making profits. The people I have met while owning and working at Weber Advertising will always have a special place in my heart.

This book is also dedicated to the Sisters of St. Joseph of the Apparition and Rodney Merard. The factory doesn't happen without a remarkable group of supporters who have their "boots on the ground".

"Where there is no work,
there is no dignity."
Pope Francis

Contents

"Charity is injurious unless
it helps the recipient to
become independent of it."
John D. Rockefeller

Preface

We always expected a ripple effect, but not to this degree. Shortly after our factory's first anniversary, we were surprised to see the degree to which our factory was able to combat poverty for thousands of people who lived close to our factory. Life got better for neighbors as the ripple effect from payroll lifted many across the UN's extreme poverty line. Relatively, our employees did extremely well as they experienced paydays that were 500% larger than their neighbors. Also, it should be noted that there is a difference between combating hunger which is achieved through providing food and combating poverty which is achieved by providing opportunity. This is not a feel-good story but instead a manual on how 100+ jobs lifted thousands of people out of extreme poverty. We also wanted to bring to light the mistakes we made so they may be avoided by ourselves and others in the future.

There are certain themes in this book that are redundant in nature and that was done purposely so a reader can get the general concepts by reading 3 or 4 chapters. At the reader's choosing, they can dig into more detail by reading all of the chapters and skimming through the parts that are deemed redundant.

It is the author's desire to build interest for combating poverty, as well as combating hunger, and to advance the Economic Mission concept in other extremely poor communities. Our factory made polo shirts. This Economic Mission model is scalable because the

US market demands over 500 million polo shirts each year. This Economic Mission model can also be replicated and Economic Mission factories could be competitive by manufacturing anything that is labor-intensive.

This book briefly discusses the nature of world poverty, hunger, and poverty relief. We discuss how our Economic Mission is a less expensive, more permanent and more encompassing answer to world poverty. We discuss what we did to succeed and what we did wrong. We will break down our Economic Mission into the core functions. By drilling down into each section of our business, you may gain perspective. We believe this book defines a clear path for combating poverty. We will also present ways to replicate our Economic Mission model in hundreds of places throughout the world. Our goal is not to control the concept of Economic Missions. We need to see a world with hundreds of Economic Missions pulling hundreds of extremely impoverished communities out of poverty.

Jennifer, my wife, who is notably smarter than I, has told me to also include little stories about my experience with our first factory. She says that it will make the book more interesting. Although I want to entertain, the purpose of this book is to provide sustainable strategies and tactics so other "like minded" people can understand how to lift entire communities out of hopeless poverty. The Economic Mission concept goes far past hunger relief and can be a sustainable end to hopeless poverty for thousands of people.

Important Note:

On September 16, 2022, hundreds of AK-47 wielding thugs attacked our Economic Mission and factory which was located on the grounds of St. Joseph School and Convent in Praville, Haiti. They also destroyed the school and convent, stealing almost everything and causing over $3.5 million in damages. According to Haitian news outlets and reports, the gang was hired by Youri Latortue, a former senator who now wants to run for the presidency in Haiti. Since the factory was on "Catholic grounds" we got caught in his attempt to destroy the Catholic Church in Gonaives, Haiti. I am told that this was in retaliation for the Catholic Church not supporting his run for the presidency. On the same day, he also destroyed the Cathedral, multiple Catholic Schools, multiple feeding centers and food banks.

Haiti has one of the world's most corrupt governments with politicians and crooked businessmen working together to line their pockets with money that was intended for good. This is evidenced by the PetroCaribe scandal where politicians fraudulently pocketed 10% of Haiti's GDP without a single arrest. These same government officials pocketed billions intended for earthquake relief in 2010. In Haiti, crooked politicians need the populace to be drastically weakened so they can continue their corrupt management of the government. Haitian officials and power brokers intentionally keep the

Caption: Before September 16, the factory was an economic engine for the people of Praville. Clearly, extreme poverty in Praville, Haiti was in decline as payroll dollars saturated the market each Friday. Since we were the only significant employer in Praville, our employees and neighbors reverted back to extreme poverty.

masses starving and uneducated as evidenced by the attack on our factory and the Catholic education system. There will be no arrests from the attack, as Haitian politicians remain unconcerned about the pain and starvation caused by their greed and incompetence

This attack on our factory will force us to do business differently. Our goal is to begin operations in other countries where people are living in extreme poverty. Our proven business model is our most valuable asset and that survived the attack. The hard assets will be replaced and we will continue to pull communities out of hopeless poverty in other countries.

Finally, some of the numbers in this book are estimations. For example, there are no population figures for Praville, therefore we don't know exactly how many people were helped by our mission. There is a photo in this book that shows how overpopulated the area is. When we realized that as many as 10 people live in each house, the 7,000 population number seems conservative. If we don't know the population, it is difficult to know exactly how many people are living under the UN's Extreme Poverty Line. United Nations statistics indicate that 1 in 3 Haitians are living below the Extreme Poverty Line and Praville is one of the poorest places in Haiti. With only 5% of the local population having full time work, and these workers averaging $2 -$3 per day, it is easy to extrapolate that the vast majority of Praville lives below the extreme poverty line. When we talk about listing people out of poverty, we are saying that we are listing people across the UN's $2.15 PPP per day extreme poverty line. Very few of Praville's residents, except for our employees, were living on $7 or more per day. To be clear, starving and hopeless poverty diminished, but nobody got rich.

Caption - Looting can be a family activity! In this photo, a local mom and her son are taking home a roll of black fabric after looting it from our factory.

Note - Extreme Poverty is a descriptive term used by the UN. It is the most severe type of poverty, defined by the UN as "a condition characterized by severe deprivation of basic human needs". Currently set at $2.15 per day, it is the base line where people can live. From what I have seen, living on less than $2.15 per day is a slow and painful death sentence.

"Consider it all joy, my brothers, when you encounter various trials, for you know that the testing* of your faith produces perseverance."

James 1 2-3

Map of the Property Surrounding the Factory

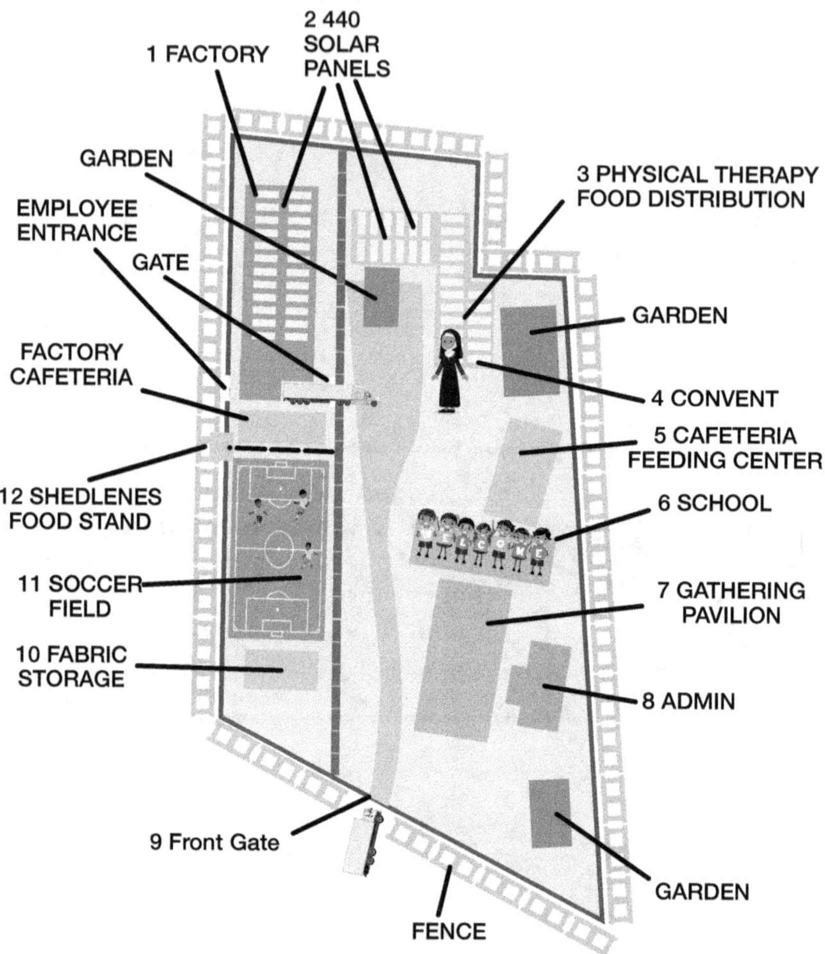

This simplified map is to provide perspective as the book is read. It was approximately 6 acres. It was a self-contained complex that sat behind 12 foot walls. Every day, 750 students attended school, food was distributed to starving families, hundreds received physical therapy and a factory was pulling employees and neighbors out of extreme poverty.

Explanation of locations on the map.

1. **Factory Area** – The factory employed 104 people. It was large and modern with a capacity of up to 1 million shirts per year. It housed state-of-the-art machinery and a very modern cutting room

2. **Solar Panels** – The factory was solar powered and we were able to provide electricity to the convent, physical therapy center, food distribution center and the school. There was no electrical grid so our solar panels did all the work.

3. **Physical Therapy Unit/Food Distribution** - In this small area, hundreds of children were receiving treatment for birth defects that came from poor prenatal conditions and other effects. Tons of food went through the food distribution unit on a monthly basis.

4. **Convent** – The convent housed 6 sisters who worked endlessly.

5. **Cafeteria** – The cafeteria provided food for every student that attended school. Often, it was the only time these children would eat each day.

6. **School** - The school provided hope. By traditional standards, the school wasn't educationally exceptional but it was the best school in the area and parents knew their children were being fed every day.

7. **Gathering Pavilion** – This seemed to be the center of everything wonderful. Kids would produce talent shows for parents, church services would take place there and special days would bring special celebrations. It was a great place to be.

8. **Administration Building** – The teachers would meet in the administration building to advance their teaching skills. The school had a minuscule operating budget which meant my factory employees were being paid better than the teachers.

9. **Front Gate** – The front gate was where the armed gang infiltrated our factory.

10. **Fabric Storage Unit** – The fabric storage unit was holding 75 miles (roughly 120,000 linear yards) of fabric on the day of the attack.

11. **Soccer Field** – The soccer field was also the playground for the school. Although it is shown as green on the map, it was really a plot of land with small stones and 2 goals. Kids loved that soccer field.

12. **Shedlene's Food Stand** – Shedlene is my favorite success story. She saw an opportunity and worked hard to make it successful. There is more on her later in the book.

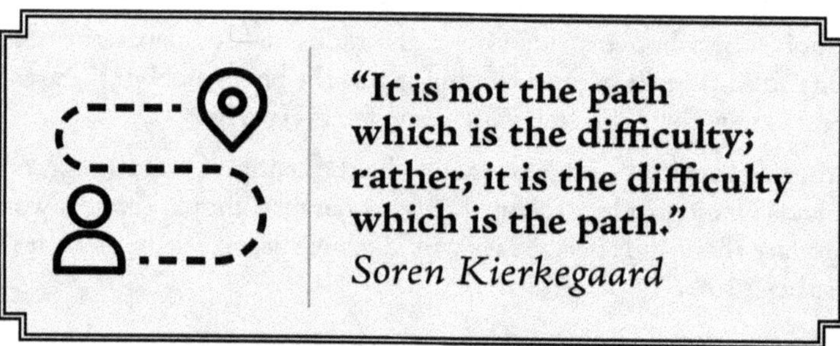
"It is not the path
which is the difficulty;
rather, it is the difficulty
which is the path."
Soren Kierkegaard

1 - What an Economic Mission Does

We believe we found the world's best way to combat extreme poverty and the horrors that go with it. You can be the judge.

A hopelessly poor community is a horrible place. However, put a factory in that community and everything changes. This is what an Economic Mission does. We lift people out of poverty by creating sustainable employment. Our factory in Haiti employed 104 people. The weekly payroll was $8,000 and that payroll caused an amazing ripple effect through town. We successfully built our factory in Praville, Haiti, which didn't have electricity or running water. Hopeless and extreme poverty affected almost everybody in the town. Our factory had a positive impact, not just for the employees, but the thousands hopelessly poor people that surrounded our factory.

Imagine the following scenario: You are a nine-year-old living with eight other people in a one-room house that is ten feet by fifteen feet. You are hungry, but your day to eat is tomorrow, not today. That's how food is rationed in Praville, Haiti. There are rat bites on your legs because you sleep on the floor and even the rats are hungry. You are also wet and dirty. It rained last night, and the cardboard in the window didn't keep out the rain, so a muddy puddle has formed where you were sleeping. You drink dirty and contaminated water, and when things turn from bad to worse, your fifteen-year-old sister sells her body for a bag of rice. Dad is long gone, and Mom tries to sell bananas on the main road but everybody wants to buy on credit that will never be paid. Life is about hunger and survival but it is mostly hopeless.

Now imagine a modern factory appears in your community. Nothing like this has been there before now. There are four hundred solar panels glistening in the hot Haitian sun. Machines can be heard over the music that plays inside. Before lunch, the employees singing at daily devotions can be heard on the street below. A truck pulls out, taking a delivery to port. Somehow, the driver gets through the bumpy and narrow streets. At night, you go over to the factory gates because it is lit and you can see your friends. Over one hundred employees are actually getting paid every Friday and making about 500% more than the average wage. These factory employees have money to spend. Mom is now selling more bananas than ever before because the workers are buying. Your sister is selling lunch to the employees, and you are all eating twice a day now. You even have clean water and may finally get a pair of shoes. Mom brought home rat poison, and you are no longer getting bit as you sleep. Without rampant starvation in the community, violence has dropped off and neighbors aren't as quick to steal. Nobody in the community is getting rich, but they aren't starving anymore either.

That is what our Economic Mission does in Haiti. We put a self-contained, solar-powered factory in the middle of one of the poorest places in the Western Hemisphere. From that factory, tons of polo shirts are produced and shipped to the US. We provide opportunities and hope for local citizens, and we let human desire and payroll do the rest. It isn't a good place to visit. There are no paved roads, electricity, or running water and the food is horrible. The employees make polo shirts like their lives depend on it. The people who are selling used clothing, bananas, clean water and other items are now doing better, and their families are no longer struggling to survive. Inside the factory, almost one hundred employees are taking home an average of $80 per week. Before their first payday, the vast majority had never even held $30 in their hand at one time in their lives. Most employees were living on $2 per day or less before working at our factory.

The Little Factory That Could

As the factory was coming together, I was telling my friends and partners that God's hands are all over this project. I firmly believe amazing things happened because I was doing God's will and I needed his help. Having God's hands on the factory made it possible but it wasn't easy. It is important to recognize that the success of the factory was a testimony to human perseverance and tenacity. Simply put, the factory was the will of God and its success was the will of local people.

Think about this. In one year, poorly educated and malnourished people became skilled laborers, made polo shirts and in their first year became competitive enough to compete in the world market with China and even sweatshops. Even the construction of the factory was a bit of a miracle. The building was able to withstand 107 mph hurricane winds and a 7.6 earthquake. We were doing business with name brands that we would all recognize. We operated in a town that didn't have electricity and not one road in Praville was paved or even named. There were no grocery stores or restaurants in Praville because nobody had money. Praville, by all measures, was one of the worst places in the Western Hemisphere.

My wonderful staff in Praville made high quality polo shirts that were comparable to any brand that would be sold in any department store. We didn't cut one corner and we didn't accept anything that wasn't perfect. These shirts looked great and felt great when being worn. The majority of our fabrics were made in America. The Fortune 500 company that was giving us orders of 25,000 polo shirts did a quality audit and after 8 hours of searching for errors, one single shirt failed because it was missing the care and content label. The miracle was that this extremely impoverished town was building a bright future by making high quality polo shirts at some of the best prices in the world. I have no doubt that if we could have continued to build momentum, we could have raised production levels to millions of polo shirts per year. Then we could have done dress shirts, pants, shoes or anything else that was labor-intensive. We could have pumped insane amounts of money into Praville and other impoverished communities. Our value proposition was exceptional because we made higher quality shirts and nobody, not even sweatshops, could beat us on price. Companies loved buying from us because they felt that they were making a difference and it didn't cost them anything to do it.

Pravi Products That Were Produced in our Praville Factory

Our Haitian factory, Grateful Inc., made polo shirts. Everything that was made in the factory was exported to the US. Our shirts sold as school and work uniforms. They also sold in retail applications and even as apparel for our local baseball team. We were able to earn contracts with an international fast food franchise and a Fortune 500 uniform company. These large entities gave us orders for as many as 50,000 shirts. We sent entire shipping containers filled with shirts to the US. A production line can produce 600 high quality shirts a day and we had 2 production lines. Producing an order of 50,000 shirts would take approximately 8 to 9 weeks of continuous production. We only needed orders for 275,000 shirts to keep our 2 production lines busy for a whole year. When we were getting 50,000 shirt orders, 275,000 shirts seemed very achievable. We were in position to need an additional production line which would have been a huge benefit to the community. With the expansion of additional production lines, payroll grew substantially. With the positive growth of payroll, our ability to lift people out of poverty increased.

My partners and I were very surprised and thrilled by how payday lifted the whole community. The ripple effect of $8,000

SIDE STORY

The Logo Explained

We chose a hummingbird enjoying the nectar of a flower as an emblem that goes with our logo and it is also embroidered on the left chest of our shirts. We named that bird "Rodney" in honor of Rodney Merard, recognizing his dedication and commitment to combating poverty in Haiti. Like the employees at our mission, the hummingbird only eats through his work of hovering over flowers while plucking the nectar. While contemplating logo options, I was looking out the window of my hotel in Port-au-Prince. I saw a hummingbird find his breakfast from a bed of flowering weeds that were outside my window. Like our employees, there wasn't much opportunity for that hummingbird. Like our employees, he took advantage of his opportunity and because of that, he ate and lived life.

being injected into an impoverished community of about 7,000 was amazing, but looking back, it could have been easily predicted. The weekly routine injection of that cash was extremely powerful. Praville was an isolated and extremely poor community, so on payday almost every dollar that was spent by our employees was being re-spent by extremely poor people almost as soon as it was received. This was very beneficial to the extremely poor neighbors. A dollar didn't sit in pockets in Praville. As an employee bought shoes for their kids (used shoes from the US), the person that received that dollar was immediately spending it because they had very hungry kids. When the food vendor got paid, it was spent immediately on clean water. It was a chain reaction. Although our employees enjoyed having the basics, each time they gave a dollar to somebody, it was almost always immediately spent. It was crazy. A dollar spent on Saturday morning could be used and re-spent 10 times or more by Saturday evening. More importantly, that dollar that was spent on Saturday morning helped non-employees over and over again. That was the beauty of our Economic Mission and my partners and I loved it. We actually grew to love paydays because we knew the power of paydays. We significantly improved the lives of thousands of people, one payday at a time.

Dollars Don't Stay Forever

Eventually dollars left the Praville community, but not before they did their job of improving life over and over again. As street vendors replenish their supplies and as people venture out into the broader area, dollars flow out of the neighborhood economy. A portion of the payroll also leaves as employees sent money to family members who live far away. Although the dollars leaving the market still improve someone's life, the impact is limited since they don't accumulate to a critical mass nor do they have the same powerful ripple effect. We also discussed micro-financing for small businesses so payroll dollars would stay in Praville longer, thereby amplifying our ripple effect. Dollars will leave the market but a new payday was always around the corner and a new wave of dollars will hit the streets.

Additionally, we stumbled upon another phenomenon that greatly aided us. We didn't plan it this way, but because of our mission partners, many overhead costs like rent, loan payments and utilities were non-existent. This phenomenon gave us an enormous competitive advantage in the world market. Essentially, we could provide our workers with significantly better wages while maintaining the world's lowest prices. We call this phenomenon "Vacated Expenses". Large orders came from companies who liked our mission and loved that we could also be a low-cost supplier. Because so many of our expenses were vacated or nonexistent, we only basically paid for raw materials, transportation, and labor. We didn't have utilities, rent, bank interest, or import tax payments. Furthermore, we are

the wonderful effects of
The High Speed Dollar
One dollar can routinely help 9 people in 21 hours

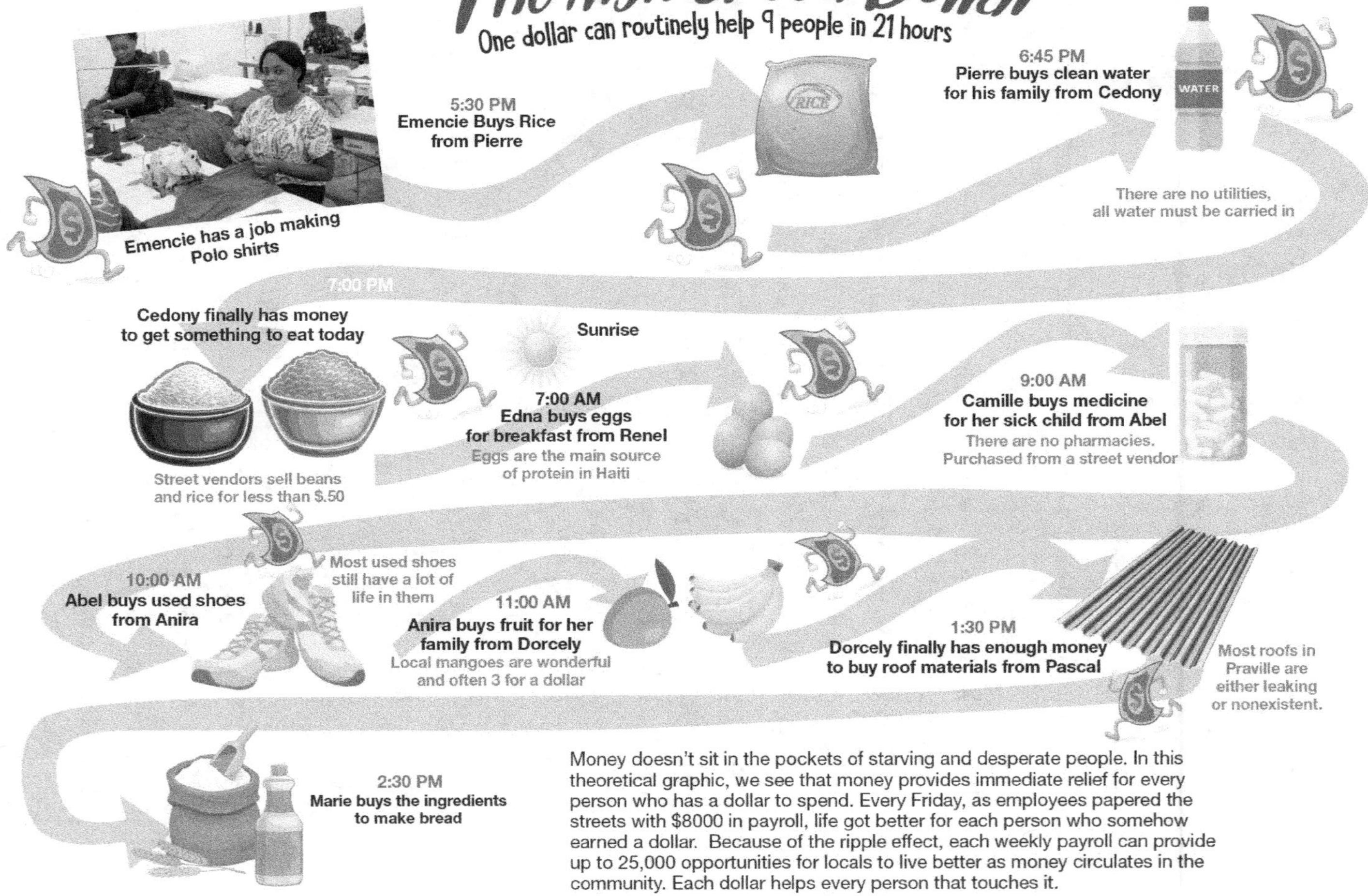

Emencie has a job making Polo shirts

5:30 PM
Emencie Buys Rice from Pierre

6:45 PM
Pierre buys clean water for his family from Cedony
There are no utilities, all water must be carried in

7:00 PM

Cedony finally has money to get something to eat today
Street vendors sell beans and rice for less than $.50

Sunrise

7:00 AM
Edna buys eggs for breakfast from Renel
Eggs are the main source of protein in Haiti

9:00 AM
Camille buys medicine for her sick child from Abel
There are no pharmacies. Purchased from a street vendor

10:00 AM
Abel buys used shoes from Anira
Most used shoes still have a lot of life in them

11:00 AM
Anira buys fruit for her family from Dorcely
Local mangoes are wonderful and often 3 for a dollar

1:30 PM
Dorcely finally has enough money to buy roof materials from Pascal
Most roofs in Praville are either leaking or nonexistent.

2:30 PM
Marie buys the ingredients to make bread

Money doesn't sit in the pockets of starving and desperate people. In this theoretical graphic, we see that money provides immediate relief for every person who has a dollar to spend. Every Friday, as employees papered the streets with $8000 in payroll, life got better for each person who somehow earned a dollar. Because of the ripple effect, each weekly payroll can provide up to 25,000 opportunities for locals to live better as money circulates in the community. Each dollar helps every person that touches it.

currently in an era where companies prioritize social and environmental responsibility. Large companies love our solar-paneled factory that was built specifically for lifting people out of poverty. It made getting appointments and closing sales easier. We will discuss this later in this book.

We believe that we possess another crucial competitive advantage. Our Economic Mission is doing the will of God, and it is for Him that we sweat. The hand of God is all over our mission, and that is our best advantage. Even after the terroristic destruction, we feel we have an opportunity to rebuild in another country where there is a government and do great things on a bigger scale. We perceive the terrorist attack as an unfortunate aspect of conducting business in Haiti. We learned and we can grow from our Haitian experience. Everything we need comes from God helping us to do His will. We have prayed for money, technological experts, great management, and even large contracts, and our prayers always get answered. We feel like God is our partner, and He is not a silent partner. It feels odd claiming God's will as a competitive advantage, but there are other times in the Bible where God has been an advantage. Ask Moses when you see him.

Why Polo Shirts???

Is it crazy to have a factory that can only produce polo shirts? We think not. In fact, we aren't sure there is another line of business that would be preferred. There are 530 million polo shirts purchased in the USA every year. We are uniquely positioned to become a significant player in the manufacturing of polo shirts. We can make polos well and we can also be the low cost supplier. As we grow, we will also benefit from a larger scale operation which would make us even more cost competitive. Further, we can service US businesses better and faster because we are closer than China, Vietnam or India. Finally, the ownership is more personal than a faceless international commodity company. We will be more responsive and enjoy better personal relationships with our customers. We can do smaller custom runs, in person sales calls and make customers feel great about their relationship with us. We see no reason why we can't evolve into an operation that sells 25 million shirts per year.

Manufacturing polo shirts enables us to make a significant positive impact. If we produced one million polo shirts, that would be a market share of less than two-tenths of one percent. When we get to producing a million polos, we will be able to employ more than two hundred people, which will allow us to put $16,000 of payroll on the streets each Friday. That would make an enormous difference in any local community where we would operate. As one of the world's lowest-cost suppliers of quality polo shirts, we believe a one percent market share is reachable in the relative short term. If we could get to one percent market share, or 5.3 million shirts, we could employ about 1,100 people, and our weekly payroll would exceed $85,000. For a Third World community, a weekly injection of $85,000 would improve lives in unimaginable ways. And that is just polo shirts. This model can produce pants, oxford shirts, toothbrushes, auto parts, and just about anything else that is labor intensive.

The photo above was taken about 2 months before the factory was being completed. For the people of Praville, the factory was a beacon of hope. It was the source of a brightening economic picture and something that benefited the whole town.

We made our mistakes, and we encountered tons of obstacles. We made errors when hiring people and ordering equipment. We opened just before the COVID crisis, and we had enormous supply chain nightmares. We started operating during history's worst shipping crisis. Our shipping delays were massive, and shipping costs often doubled or tripled. By simply mentioning that we opened a factory in Haiti, we could evoke sympathy from almost any international businessman. The governmental officials that are responsible for bringing companies to Haiti tried to extort $50,000 from us. (We didn't pay.) Gangs are infesting Haiti like cockroaches, and basics like gasoline or fresh water are always in short supply. In spite of this, we succeeded. Again, God's hands are all over this mission, and He sent us wonderful support via the

Sisters of Saint Joseph of the Apparition to help us, as well as my friend Rodney.

We never wanted to let the failure go to waste without learning from it. It was important that we didn't make the same mistakes twice. We learned that the daily obstacles we faced were not in the way. The obstacles became opportunities for us to enhance and expand our capabilities. As we attacked obstacles and problems, we had better opportunities and systems as a payoff. Learning from mistakes and clearing obstacles helped us increase our production numbers. The obstacles made us better. We would say that the only difference between us and Nike is that they have cleared a lot more obstacles.

Finally, it is important to note that a system of Economic Missions does not mean the 100% end of all poverty worldwide, but we proved in Praville, Haiti, that this Economic Mission model works. Our factory pulled an entire community out of hopeless poverty and mass starvation. Nobody gets rich, but nobody starves either. Our model worked in a country that was governed by buffoons and is reported to be the most corrupt country in the western half of the world. Our model works in the worst conditions. We proved that it is possible to drastically improve life for 7,000 people by employing 104 people. After reading this, it would be my hope that you would be motivated to do whatever you can. I would surely help!

God delivered faster than Dominoes

It was a frightening end to a very good day. Our factory was coming together and even looked like the drawings said it would. It was time to order sewing machines and the solar power plant. It was 3 PM and I called the sewing machine dealer to put in my order for 70 machines. It was only then that I learned that there were different kinds of machines and they had to be configured differently for different uses. Further, I had to figure out the solar energy component and all of the other mechanical details of the factory. I was desperate. Just before dinner, I prayed for a solution to my problem and then I went for dinner at the hotel restaurant. As I was enjoying my "delightful dinner" of hot dogs in ketchup on spaghetti noodles, my prayers were answered. In the middle of nowhere, I met the Apaids who happened to be the owners of one of Haiti's largest textile facility. They appreciated my mission and they gave me the services of Gilbert Durand, their top engineer, until my factory was up and running. My prayer was answered in less than 30 minutes.

"If you want happiness for a year, inherit a fortune. If you want happiness for a lifetime, help someone else."
Confucius

2 – ABOUT POVERTY

We should hate hopeless poverty far more than we do.

This experience will impact my life forever. I was in Haiti conducting site research at the location where the factory would soon be built. With twenty minutes and with nothing to do, I decided to visit the feeding center and play with a few kids. My "happy time" was harshly interrupted by the horrific screams of a mother carrying her child, who was dying from starvation. The look of horror, desperation, and despair on the mother's face still haunts me. I wish I could remove that horrific image from my memory. It was the lifeless angelic face and the way his tiny lifeless arms and legs dangled from his mother's arms that permanently changed my life. There is a horrific ugliness that lingers long after seeing something like this. This was the exact moment when I made the decision to give up my comfortable job at an advertising agency and become an economic missionary. This was the exact moment when my head connected to my heart and all of the statistics had faces.

People, Not Numbers

Perhaps the ugliest sin that rests on mankind is how we let 648 million citizens of our world live in hopeless poverty and basically "die in place". Imagine living below the UN's Extreme Poverty Line of $2.15 per day. People who live below the extreme poverty line aren't able to acquire what they need to stay alive and therefore, they are dying in a slow and painful manner. Over 25% of the global population lives on less than $3.20 per day. Half of the world lives on less than $5.50 per day. Too often, a self-centered, dualistic perspective is taken, where it becomes a scenario of "them" who live in poverty and "us" who are fortunate enough to be born elsewhere. Our way of coping with our self-centeredness is to reduce these children of God into numbers and bar charts. Instead of focusing on starving people, we focus on ourselves by saying that we are grateful and fortunate. We don't deeply empathize for these people. Our compassion extends only as far as that satisfies our consciences and egos. We make sure it doesn't interrupt the wonderful day we are having. We hope that by recognizing that we are fortunate and grateful, we can free ourselves from our responsibility of caring for the poorest of the poor. We cannot ignore these people and still call ourselves a moral society. We must not dehumanize these people. Most of us are guilty of this on some level. I'm reluctant to admit that I once viewed third-world moms as not loving their kids as much, because they have other problems. That crashed in on me when I saw that mom wailing over her child. I too was guilty of letting the children of God become numbers and faceless bar charts. I am guilty of seeing a photo of a starving man without comprehending the violent struggle that his family indoors just to secure their next meal.

In this chapter, we will demonstrate how hopeless poverty and starvation in the world are in decline. It is a brightening picture where people are climbing out of the worst forms of poverty. But these statistics don't mean anything to a starving child. When that mom buried her child, she wasn't taking solace in the fact that the per capita GDP was rising in poor countries around the world. That is the difference between people and numbers.

Don't get me wrong, I love numbers. I constantly review all kinds of World Bank and United Nations statistics, and surprisingly, I find them interesting. To me, the seventy-six columns and 2,300 rows of the new Social Progress Index reads like a good book. The challenge for me remains that I don't let people turn into numbers.

The good news is that as poverty numbers decline, fewer moms are burying their children who fatally died due to malnutrition's effects. According to the World Bank, the percentage of the world population living in extreme poverty decreased from 29.1% in 2000 to 8.4% in 2019. That statistic is worth celebrating as long as we recognize that we still have a long way to go. There are still 684 million people living in hopeless poverty and billions more linger only slightly above the $2.15 extreme poverty line. The reality is, as the statistics improve there is a less violent struggle for survival for millions of people. There is hope when we realize the improving statistics represent the faces and the names of God's children who are doing better. We can celebrate these statistical victories because it shows we, as a planet, are heading in the right direction. However, the statistics also show that we have a long way to go in the realms of worldwide education, healthcare and freedoms. Remember that there might be 100,000 people behind that decimal point in that statistical number. The line on a UN bar chart may represent millions who are starving to death.

The Hungry Giver

I was in Haiti as construction on the Praville factory was beginning. Haiti wasn't in the turmoil that it is today and I felt secure on the streets while traveling with a security detail. It was Saturday evening and we went to dinner in downtown Gonaives. As we were entering the restaurant, a hungry boy about 8 years old asked me for money for food. I told him that instead I would buy him anything he wanted for dinner in the restaurant. (Don't think too much of me because everything in the restaurant was cheap.) Service was slow so we got him a soda, ice cream and a few snacks while he was waiting. I liked the kid and Rodney was also entertained by translating for me. Eventually, dinner came and he asked if he could take it home. I told him that I like him as a dinner guest and I wished he could stay. He told me that Saturdays aren't his day to eat, but he was taking it home for the people in his household. The food wasn't very good but, I appreciated it more after my dinner guest left with dinner for the half of his household that eats on Saturdays.

Combating Poverty vs. Combating Hunger

Feeding hungry people doesn't combat poverty. Poverty is the state of having an insufficient amount of necessary possessions and a low income that prohibits the acquisition of what is needed. Giving a person a bowl of vitamin fortified rice doesn't relieve the underlying causes of poverty. Efforts to combat poverty are vastly different than efforts to combat hunger. When an impoverished person is fed, they are still impoverished and they will need to be fed again tomorrow. When poverty is eliminated, these people can survive on their own. Although organizations and efforts that feed impoverished people are necessary, the vast majority of those people will continue to live in poverty and will need to be fed as long as they remain poor. Combating poverty is entirely different than combating hunger. Creating opportunity is the hallmark of the goal for the Economic Mission. Combating poverty is a process that eliminates the obstacles and the root causes of deficient incomes and insufficient necessary possessions. It is the unique goal of the Economic Mission to remove the obstacles that create poverty.

Hopeless Poverty Defined.

In this book, we use the term "Hopeless Poverty" to refer to severe or extreme poverty. The Extreme Poverty Line, according to the World Bank, is defined as people living on less than $2.15 per day. After living in Praville, Haiti, hopeless seems to better describe the emotions of people who are deeply impoverished for generation after generation. A major challenge for our mission is to provide hope; so we feel that combating Hopeless Poverty is a more accurate objective. Further, by changing the verbiage to hopeless poverty, we aren't constrained by the UN's $2.15 standard. It is adjusted for inflation and PPP (Purchasing Power Parity). The dollar doesn't go as far or buy as much in some countries and goes further in other countries. The PPP addresses these fluctuations.

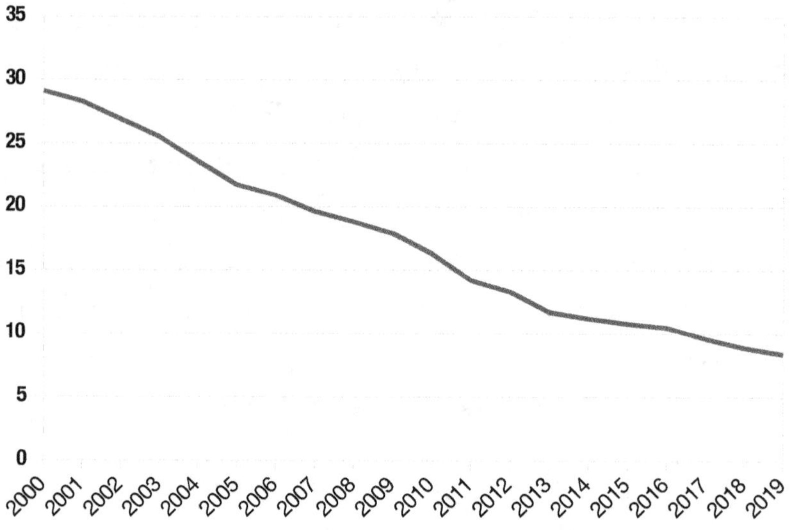

Percent of Population Living in Extreme Poverty

Poverty headcount ratio at $2.15 a day (2017 PPP) (% of population)

data.worldbank.org

This is a great chart. In the new millennium, the number of people living in extreme poverty fell by 70% from 29.1% of the population to 8.4% of the world population. There are still 648 million people living in extreme poverty.

Per Capita GDP

GDP is basically the sum of gross value added by all resident producers in the economy. There are also other small components like taxes and tariffs. Per Capita GDP is an indicator of the strength of the economy for that particular country. It is widely accepted that stronger economies means a better standard of living on average. As GDP grows, so does the standard of living. When the total size of the GDP is divided by the population, it is considered to be on a per capita basis. The Per Capita GDP provides a way to compare GDPs of countries of varying size. Although China's GDP is much higher than Ireland, Ireland's per capita GDP is much higher than China. On the aggregate, China produces more but Ireland can boast of a better Standard of Living. It is important to note that this chart adjusts for inflation by presenting all values in 2015 dollars.

GDP Per Capita Basis - Selected Caribbean & Central American Countries

Poverty headcount ratio at $2.15 a day (2017 PPP) (% of population)

data.worldbank.org

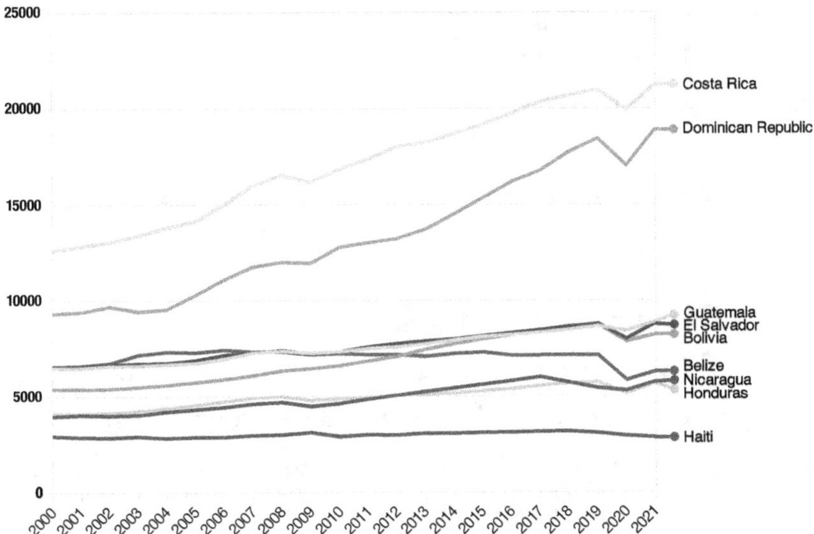

In the millennium, Per Capita GDP continued to grow on a steady basis, except for the dips for the 2008 recession and the COVID Pandemic. It is important to note the Per Capita GDP was resilient after the dips.

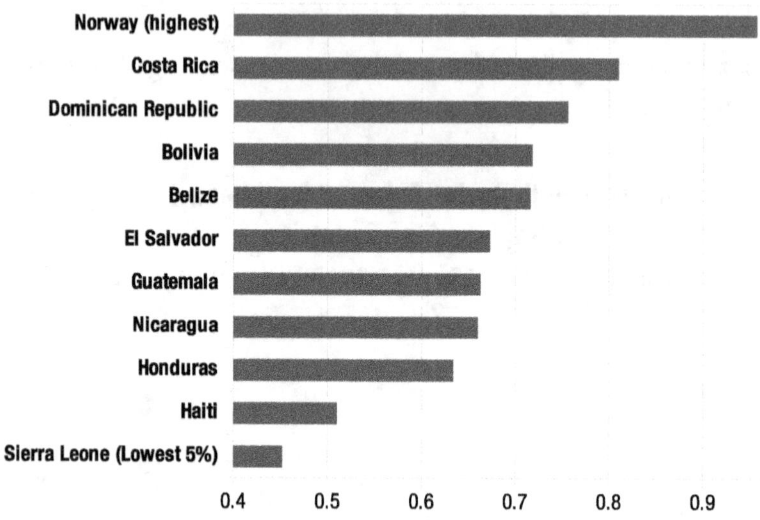

The Human Development Index provides a picture that is about more than money as it considers education and health as well.

Human Development Index (HDI)

Because life is about more than money, we have the HDI ratings. This index comes from the UN and indexes countries based on health and knowledge as well as a nation's financial strength. HDI is a more complete picture of life in a country. It should be noted that for people in hopeless poverty, the immediate need of feeding themselves will take precedence over the other components of the HDI score.

Extreme Poverty Versus Relative Poverty

I hear it all the time. Well meaning people suggest that US has poverty and I don't need to leave the country to combat poverty. They are correct if they are saying that the US has people who are poor relative to other people who live in the same town and share the same streets. The good news is that the US doesn't have extreme poverty as defined by the UN. If there is poverty to this degree in the US, it is very rare and I have never seen or heard about it. Poor Americans experience hunger, but I haven't seen starvation in the US. I have never read an article reporting people starving to death in Philadelphia or any other city. I have never seen a child with a distended stomach in the US while it is commonplace in Haiti. In Haiti, the kids will eat a cookie made of flour and mud. I have not seen that in the US. In Haiti, the root cause of extreme poverty is clearly the lack of opportunity. This isn't the case in the US.

Extreme Poverty Defined

Until recently, the World Bank had the extreme poverty line at $1.90 per day using 2011 dollars. Adjusted for inflation, the new World Bank Extreme Poverty Line is now $2.15. This is calculated on a PPP (Purchasing Power Parity) basis using 2017 dollars. There is severe and threatening deprivation for anyone living below $2.15. In 2019, there were 648 million people (8.4% of the world population) living at or below the extreme poverty line. Simple research indicates that the worst poverty in the world is in Africa. In Haiti, the Western Hemisphere's poorest country, almost 30%

of the population lives in extreme poverty according to the World Bank. Haiti's daily per capita GDP is less than $5 per day and NPR called Haitians making $3 per day "high earners" in a relative sense. Other poor countries like Belize or Guatemala have a daily per capita GDP is $12 to $14. It is important to remember that GDP isn't average income but instead an aggregate production value that indicates the economy's strength. Countries like Belize have 53.7% of their population living under $5.50 per day according to the World Bank. We believe that any area where the general population is living on $2.75 per day or less could greatly benefit from an Economic Mission. The benefit of our Economic Mission grows in disproportion to the area's depth of poverty. For example, in Praville, Haiti, an employee earning $15 a day makes 500% - 700% more than the typical employee. In Belize or Guatemala, that same $15 is only 300% better than what the typical worker makes. Obviously both would benefit, but the poorer Haitian community benefits more from an Economic Mission.

In countries like Haiti, Honduras or Sierra Leone, there are no safety nets. Countries with mass hopeless poverty cannot have food banks or other safety nets, because demand for food and other services would wipe out any institution in minutes, or hours at best. Feeding programs led by NGOs (Non-Governmental Organizations/Aid Organizations) choose between helping a limited few and feeding many without consistently helping anybody. My experience indicates that most NGOs put most of their efforts into helping a chosen group of people at the unfortunate cost of excluding others. This choice comes down to tough economic decisions that are dictated by the scarcity of resources. In the US or other developed countries, food banks and other services can prevent starvation and extreme poverty as defined by the UN. Developed countries have more governmental and organizational resources. Further, the people being helped in developed countries are almost always above the UN extreme poverty line.

I love this picture. Daphne was a great student in our sewing school. With her mom, she took remnant fabric from our factory and made this dress for Christmas. In spite of hunger and language barriers, she always lit up the room I promised her a job as soon as labor laws would permit.

Relative Poverty Defined:

People in relative poverty live far better than people in extreme poverty. In the US, the poverty line for one person is $13,590, or $37.23 a day. In countries with extreme poverty, people would have to live for seventeen days on the same $37.23 that an impoverished American lives on for one day. Relative to the median US income of $44,000, people earning $13,590 are relatively poor. However, these same people are relatively rich compared to people living in extreme poverty. There are some zip codes in the United States where kids think they are poor because they didn't get a new car for graduation. I have not seen extreme poverty in the US. This doesn't mean we shouldn't try to improve the human condition for our poorest fellow citizens. It means that poor citizens of other countries have a significantly lower standard of living than there is in the US

Thoreau in the Third World?

Consider Henry David Thoreau's famous quote as it relates to developed and impoverished economies. This example defines the difference between extreme poverty versus relative poverty. His famous quote from Walden was that "The mass of men lead lives of quiet desperation." It paints life as a world of bored people desperately relying on their paychecks so they can pay bills, mortgages and work towards retirement. When that doesn't happen, Americans quietly and desperately turn towards the great safety net where they are fed and housed by government institutions and well-financed not-for-profit entities. It's different for people living in extreme poverty. In countries where extreme poverty exists, the mass of men lead lives of violent desperation. People in extreme poverty desperately do whatever they need to do so they can exist for one more day. If that means selling their daughter into prostitution or stealing food from an old lady, that is what is done. Quiet desperation implies endless boredom while violent desperation implies hopeless suffering and that is the difference between extreme and relative poverty.

SIDE STORY

Dieufferson would like it!!!

In order to make my flight the next day, I had to leave our Haitian factory and spend the night in Port-au-Prince. I stayed at the Servotel hotel for security reasons. The hotel has been in decline. The telephone, several lights and outlets were not working. There wasn't soap in the bathroom, the TV didn't work and the carpeting was badly worn. The prepaid breakfast was also in decline featuring toast, local fruit and cereal. At breakfast, I was complaining to Rodney about the hotel conditions when Dieufferson, my director of security at the factory, walks in grinning ear to ear. I asked Rodney to translate and ask why Dieufferson was so happy; Dieufferson replied that the hotel was amazing. It had running water, a toilet that flushed, most of the lights worked and it was the first night in his life he slept in air-conditioning. He also said the breakfast buffet was amazing because it had several choices. Since that time, when things aren't right at a hotel where I am staying, my wife or I will say "Dieufferson would like it" and that reminds us how good we have it.

Causes of Poverty

There are many causes of poverty in the world. This section will address the main root causes that I have seen in Haiti. It will also address poverty issues in the United States.

The Root Cause of Haitian Poverty

In Haiti, the bulk of hopeless poverty is caused by a lack of opportunity. I saw an interview with Warren Buffett and they asked him what he did to become so wealthy. Mr Buffett basically said the first thing he did was to be born in the right place and to the right parents. The people born in Praville, Haiti, are living in the exact opposite circumstance. In Praville, there is no opportunity and almost all children live in single-parent households where a woman is trying to help her children survive. Although I made a nice living in the US, I don't know how I could have fed myself if I was born in Haiti. There is almost no opportunity to succeed, nor is there an opportunity to leave. Many Haitians have passports that are worthless because every country demands a visa as well as a passport to leave Haiti. Even with a visa, it is virtually impossible for Haitians to get a work permit. Extremely low employment rates at 5%–10% means that employers can pay as little as they want and people line up for those jobs. Since Haitians have no opportunity and no ability to leave Haiti, personal poverty is almost automatic.

The largest obstacle to opportunity in Haiti is the people who hold power within the government. They are primarily the cause of poverty in Haiti. The Haitian PetroCaribe scandal involved

Venezuela providing oil at a drastically reduced cost with billions of profits to be allocated to improve infrastructure and life in Haiti. Instead, government officials pocketed $2 billion of aid and Venezuela never got paid either. $2 billion is approximately 10% of Haiti's gross domestic product, and there were no arrests. In 2010, an earthquake hit Haiti; 250,000 people died, and millions of people experienced significant damage to their homes. As $13.5 billion arrived in Haiti, government officials and powerbrokers stuffed their pockets. In Haiti, crooked politicians need the populace to be drastically weakened so they can continue their corrupt management of the government. If there was a middle class, this fraud and embezzlement could not happen. If there was a police force and culture of justice, government officials would be held in check. It is a habit of Haitian government officials to beg for their country then steal for themselves when the aid arrives. When possible, they will also use foreign aid as a tool to gain power. Because of a well embedded culture of corruption, businesses cannot survive in a crime-infested marketplace. Without commerce, there is no opportunity, and poverty is omnipresent. This is evidenced by the fact that Coca-Cola produces almost 300% more revenue than the entire Haitian population of 11.5 million people.

The poverty causing obstacles in third world countries are different than the obstacles that cause poverty in the United States. Since people in third world countries need opportunity, Economic Missions are a wonderful option. Economic Missions provide an opportunity for employees to make a living where the basic needs are secure and it offers opportunity to the community that surrounds the mission. The US has different obstacles to their relative poverty problem and those problems require a different solution. This is why an Economic Mission in the US won't be effective. Economic Missions are most effective in hopelessly impoverished areas and in very poor countries.

Root Causes of Relative Poverty in the US

When compared to the world's impoverished countries, the US is replete with opportunity. Because of this amount of opportunity, the US is ranked toward the top in every index, including GDP and the UN's Human Development Index (HDI). The US poverty line is seventeen times higher than what the World Bank defines as poverty. As a wealthy country, the US spends an average of over $13,000 per student per year on education. Disappointingly, after these expenditures, there are still 59 million Americans who rely on the government for food and housing. Inner city grocery stores report that public assistance payments are involved in as many as 50% – 75% of their transactions. College students, after receiving even more education, can't pay their bills and are asking the government to bail them out. With the world's largest economy and an enormous investment in education, we must ask ourselves why we have so many people failing and unable to take care of themselves. What obstacles are causing our relative poverty? In his 1964 State of the Union Address, Lyndon Johnson declared a "war on poverty" that quickly morphed into a war on personal responsibility.

Do We Create Our Root Causes of Poverty?

I believe we do on at least some extent. I propose that a significant part of the US poverty problem is cultural. The Brookings Institute refers to a "Success Sequence," where students first graduate, then secure a steady job, then marry before having children; as a solid strategy to avoid poverty. In fact, according to the Institute for Family Studies website, people who adhere to the Success Sequence have a 97% chance of living above the US government's poverty line. Deviating from the parameters of the Success Sequence has its costs. Numerous studies demonstrate that the risk of living in poverty is 500% greater for single parents. A single parent often can't stay late to assist their company when it is needed and single parents tend to take more sick days due to illness and other childcare responsibilities. Most would agree that these actions are commendable. On the other hand, a parent with a support network can become a more valuable asset to their employer due to their availability during business emergencies. Further, they aren't taking as many sick days because their child is ill. With all else being equal, when it is time for a promotion, it stands to reason that any sensible business will promote the individual who was consistently available during critical periods. Our culture ignores these objective realities and hard truths but the scenarios constantly play out in our society over and over again.

Our prisons are consistently populated with high school dropouts, many of whom have learning disabilities. According to the National Library of Medicine, 47.8% of the inmates they studied demonstrated deficient performance in reading. Educators often discuss the concept of school suspensions being a pipeline to prison. It quickly becomes apparent that this "pipeline to prison" is reinforced by parental apathy and the failure of the school system to devise a creative solution for students with learning disabilities. These scenarios exemplify how poverty can be induced. Truth is, our culture, parents, government and our school system routinely accepts and perpetuates conditions that allow our students to be victimized by these and other root causes of poverty. We should be able to expect better outcomes if parents and educators worked together to help their students rise above these root causes. Instead of passing students who were not learning, what if we successfully trained students with learning disabilities to be valuable employees instead of convicts.

As a culture, we continue to live counter to what these easy-to-understand concepts prescribe. Public schools won't share this information with at risk teens. In my research, the Success Sequence rarely gets portrayed as incorrect. Instead, educators and politicians claim that it is too difficult for a student to be married and have a job before having children. The ghetto culture tolerates, and in some instances, celebrates teenage pregnancy, single-parent households and even incarcerations. These people experience the consequences of these actions and in essence get burned by the objective natural law. In the long run, it is impossible to beat the odds and when we don't, poverty follows. We feel like we can ignore the risks and forgo the basic rules of life, but that philosophy is severely wrong. Maybe there is a big difference between education and wisdom and that gap is widening.

There is a right way to manage life. Doing the right things will vastly improves the odds of living an abundant life. Doing the wrong things will diminish the odds of living in prosperity. Doing the wrong things like dropping out of school, drug use, single parenting, living the ghetto culture, committing crimes and being without skills will drastically increase the likelihood of personal American Relative Poverty. It's that simple.

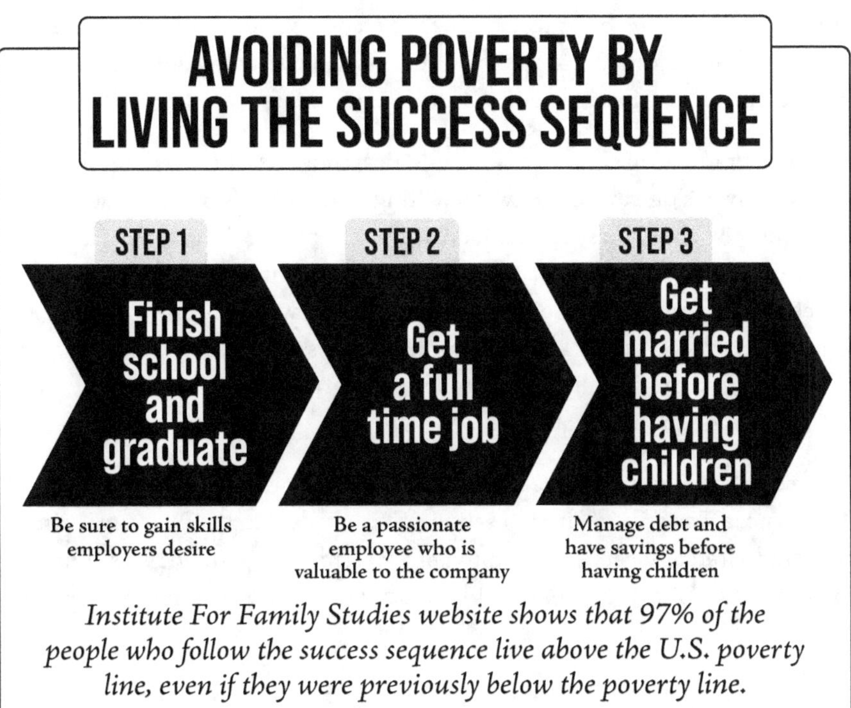

Institute For Family Studies website shows that 97% of the people who follow the success sequence live above the U.S. poverty line, even if they were previously below the poverty line.

Living the Success Sequence

Luke is my godson and I am particularly proud of him.

In high school, Luke wasn't a great student. His traditional course to college was hitting lots of bumps and his report cards and attendance records showed it. But one day, Luke decided to change that and enrolled in a diesel technology training course that the schools vo-tech was offering. Without work obligations or commitments to a spouse or child, he was free to immerse himself in his studies and became one of the top students in the diesel program and he had perfect attendance. Upon graduating, he continued to learn advanced diesel technologies at a technical school and again he loved what he did and was able to throw himself into it because he didn't have obligations. He became so accomplished, he was hired on a part-time basis to practice his trade before he even graduated. Luke completed the first step of the success sequence by graduating and he used his education to become a skilled candidate.

After graduating, Luke became a dedicated and committed employee. He was always on time and always willing to do whatever it took so his company could be successful. Again, without the obligation of a child or a wife, he could work overtime and commit himself to his new career. Luke's paychecks began to reflect that he was becoming a valuable employee. His company keeps giving him raises, he loves what he is doing and he is setting himself up for success. Congratulations on clearing the 2nd step of the success sequence.

Recently, Luke announced his engagement but there was one obstacle. His fiancée was still in nursing school. So they decided to wait until after she graduated and secured a job to get married. They are DINKs (**D**ual **I**ncomes, **N**o **K**ids) and will be able to pay off their first house in 5 years if they choose. They are in position to be financially stable and live the kind of life they desire.

This is the perfect example of how people benefit from the success sequence. The reality is that Luke made the most of each opportunity but didn't deliberately follow the success sequence. Until Luke gave me permission to use this story in my book, he had never heard of the success sequence and it seems American schools consider it politically incorrect to provide this information to students.

Consumerism is another reason why 59 million Americans rely on the government to feed and house themselves. As Americans, we buy things we don't need with money we don't have to impress people we don't even know. This gets us into trouble. Consumerism is another way for people who live in the wealthy land of opportunity to slip into relative poverty. According to a Federal Reserve report, 40% of Americans "would have difficulty handling an emergency expense as small as $400." Somehow Americans are convinced that Air Jordan sneakers and new cars with their big payments can make them happy. Rent to own companies, that used to rent TVs and appliances are now renting Coach handbags and Invicta watches. The online example I found featured a handbag renting for $10 a week for 42 weeks. If a handbag needs to be financed with payments being made on a weekly basis, a $420 designer handbag is way too expensive. This is one example of how our poorest Americans pay the most exorbitant interest rates and seem to get the worst deals from banks, credit cards and predatory sales organizations.

The poor become poorer when they buy things they don't need, with money they don't have.

Companies like banks, credit card companies and popular brands like Nike line up to take advantage of the poorest Americans. These companies understand the culture and how to use it to maximize profits. Hollywood and professional athletes are grabbing millions of dollars to get our most gullible Americans to spend money they don't have on the products they don't need. I recently saw Michael Jordan's yacht. It didn't take long for me to recognize that his yacht wasn't purchased solely on money that was earned as a basketball player. Clearly, Nike and Michael Jordan cashed in on a poor and ignorant culture whose kids needed Air Jordan sneakers for the first day of school.

Are We Living Wrong?

The need for "stuff" has replaced wisdom and virtue. It is sad to realize that one out of eight citizens from the world's biggest economy can't buy their own milk at the grocery store. The culture of consumerism has kicked aside the sage advice of ancient philosopher Epictetus who said, "Wealth consists not in having great possessions but in having few wants." We no longer trust God. We trust celebrities who dictate what we should buy and what we should think. They tell us that we can break all the laws of common sense and still be OK. Is American poverty in part the result of abandoning objective truth and wisdom? Albeit, not in all cases, but a case is easily made that American consumerism is detrimental to the welfare of our citizens, with the poor getting hurt the most. My grandparents and their parents had less opportunity, less technology and less money but they survived and lived good lives. Their survival mechanism was their ability to live within their means. My grandparents possessed wisdom and they didn't spend 20% of their take-home pay on cable TV. To them, spending extra money on DoorDash would be a sign of laziness. America remains the land of opportunity and we should be mindfully taking advantage of that.

As a society, many of us lack personal discipline therefore we are unable to "delay gratification". Instead, we fall prey to our impulses and we continue to sacrifice our futures so we can have what we want today. The generations that went before us saw the enslaving nature of debt. Today, advertising campaigns make debt sound smart and easy. They tell us to buy things we don't need and we foolishly fall for it. As a society we aren't fooled. It's really an excuse. We buy into advertising claims because we now have an excuse for immediate gratification. It is almost unbelievable that a financially struggling car shopper will let a commissioned sales person tell them that they can afford the higher payment. A $65,000 car with $1,200 heated seats simply doesn't make sense for typical households. While working part-time college graduates put $80 cases of beer in the trunk of a new car and wonder why they can't pay their student loans. Recent research shows that nearly half of 21 o 34-year-old adults are living with their parents. Is this so they have more money to accumulate more stuff? That's embarrassing. We pay our celebrities and athletes whatever they ask by accepting $500 concert tickets and $300 NFL ticket prices. These are examples of people spending money they don't have to buy things they don't need to impress people they don't know.

Our culture of consumerism isn't the sole cause of poverty, but it does contribute to our problem. If our culture emphasized adhering to the Success Sequence, living modestly, avoiding debt, embracing wisdom and using our education, millions would drift from governmental dependency to dignity. That would be a healthier culture. It is recognized that there will always be relative poverty in America. Other causes of relative poverty surely include long-term diseases, violent economic downturns like the Great Depression, and catastrophic events like hurricanes. These people get saved by our great safety net. Even in these situations, many people of robust character are able to fight their way back to self-sufficiency and dignity.

Why an Economic Missions Can't Succeed in the US

An Economic Mission in the United States couldn't be effective. The main benefit an Economic Mission provides is opportunity. America is still the land of opportunity and employees who are valuable to their companies generally succeed. A lack of opportunity isn't the main cause of relative poverty in the US, but it is in Haiti and other 3rd world countries. Economic Mission employees train without getting paid and earn salaries that are much lower than US minimum wages. Ironically, the employees of the Economic Mission in Praville were making significantly more than their neighbors.

Nobody in America wants the 3rd world salary which allows the Economic Mission to compete with Chinese companies.

Because of the comparative wealth in the United States, hourly rates for labor are much higher than the rest of the world. This is a positive thing as our average laborer earns more than the vast majority of other laborers in the world. The textile industry in the US is in decline because US companies, with their high labor costs, can't compete with other countries in this labor-intensive manufacturing segment. Clothing can't be made affordably in the US where workers are making incomes that are significantly higher than their competitors. It is for these reasons that our Economic Mission is most successful in hopelessly impoverished areas where starvation is a reality.

"People were created to be loved. Things were created to be used. The reason why the world is in chaos is because things are being loved and people are being used."
Dalai Lama

The Amazon Habit and Remedy

It's a new spin on consumerism. I fight it and a lot of my friends and associates fight it. I see something or have a desire for something and I seek hyper-immediate gratification by reaching for my cell phone and buying it on Amazon. It's fast and feels almost free because I don't even need to type in my card number. My compulsion is cooking gadgets and equipment. I justify my purchases by saying things like "I rarely eat out so this is a good investment" or that I pay my credit card bill each month. I need to put this bad habit on a short leash. Here is the remedy to the Amazon habit. It is basic old-school gratification delay. I now save items that I am considering to my shopping list for at least 4 days. When 4 days are up, I go back and ask myself if I really want that item and more than 50% of the time the answer is "NO". I have saved a ton of money, and it gets easier because I realize that I almost never need, or even really want, the impulse items for which I was shopping.

The good news is that the data clearly provides evidence that hopeless poverty is declining. In spite of this improvement, we have a long way to go. For people in extreme poverty, charts have no meaning, but as people are lifted out of poverty, the world becomes a better place. In the US, our course to reducing relative poverty is quite clear, but not easy. We need to change the cultural habits and live with wisdom. As we do our part to eliminate poverty in the US and abroad, we become better people.

3 - THE ECONOMIC MISSION BUSINESS MODEL

We pay employees much better while still offering customers quality products at the lowest prices.

We may be the only entity in the world that does what we do. We want to be the big factory with a big heart! We want to locate densely populated and hopelessly impoverished communities. We then desire to build modern factories in that community. It's not just about the people working in our factory. It is our goal to employ enough people that we can pull the entire community out of hopeless (extreme) poverty through a ripple effect of our employees spending their payroll. We want to become very good at making specific items that are in high demand from US companies. We narrow our scope with the hopes of becoming very good at making one very specific product at each factory. For example, our factory in Haiti used wicking polyester fabric to make solid colored, 3 button polos with a "self collar" and stamped neck label. In other words, we wanted to be the best in the world at making a very specific product. When we ventured from our specific lane, we had inefficiencies, errors and heartache.

By narrowing our scope, we could favorably compete with sweatshops and routinely offer better prices and superior quality. We also are able to offer better turnaround times because shipping from the

Caribbean and Central America takes days compared to the Asian Pacific Rim. In order to accomplish these goals, we need the benefits that come from being a large-scale operation. In Praville, we became competitive when we had two production lines, but our costs would have further declined as we added additional production lines.

We paid the employees, whom we extensively trained, up to 500% of an estimated average income that is earned in the community. We embrace technology to make us more competitive. We manufactured polo shirts exclusively, but there is a long list of other labor intensive products where the Economic Mission business model can deliver value and be competitive in the world market place. No matter what product is being manufactured, when employees spend their weekly paychecks, the entire community is lifted as our payroll dollars touch hand after hand, helping each person who spends each dollar. We do this because it is God's will. Building a factory where there is no opportunity and having payroll help lift an entire community out of poverty is the essence of what our Economic Mission does.

Training Employees

People are the biggest factor in determining the success of a business. Ambitious people with great attitudes made the difference for our factory in Haiti. While businessmen in the US saw the obstacle of having untrained and poorly educated employees, we were able to see it differently. This was a once in a lifetime opportunity for a full-time job. Our employees worked like their lives depended on it, because it did. Our Economic Mission was their ticket out of extreme poverty. Further, they all understood that not only could they feed themselves, but they could become heroes as they helped lift thousands of their neighbors out of extreme poverty. We felt that if people in extreme poverty would do anything to feed themselves, learning to make polo shirts would be a reasonable option. As we accepted contingent employees into our training program, I envisioned them saying to their families, "We can eat every day and even twice a day if I can only learn how to work a sewing machine." The response from the families would have to be, "Do whatever it takes to be successful". We were fortunate to have had some of the most highly motivated trainees on the planet eager to become production workers. Because failure wasn't an option, our training program was going to work.

If God's hands were not all over our mission, this section would require a whole chapter. We got extraordinarily lucky. The United States has an organization called USAID, whose purpose is to help impoverished countries. They created a training facility in Port-au-Prince to train Haitians to sew in a production line in an effort to bolster the textile industry in Haiti. It was an impressive 6 week course and people who went through that course were valuable contributors on textile production lines. A great deal of money was spent teaching trainers and creating a curriculum. As our factory opened, the training facility closed and we were in a perfect position to hire the best trainers for our factory.

Our first production line was comprised of amazingly strong people who withstood horrible circumstances to become a team of people who could make quality polo shirts. Every Sunday at 2

PM, they would leave their hometown of Praville and ride via bus 6 hours to Port-au-Prince. They shared converted shipping containers for lodging that were almost always hotter than 95°. At 7 AM, they made their way to the training facility and in the evening returned back to get something to eat and get to bed as the sun would set. Although they received a small stipend, the conditions were not good and only very committed students made it. On Friday, they would often return home often by 11 PM, spend Saturdays with their families and on Sunday, do it all over again. They were great people who took care of each other and quickly became a tight knit team of professionals. I see them as heroes who made it possible for others to come successfully behind them.

As we were opening, it became abundantly clear that training was going to be one of the key difference makers at our Haitian factory. Attitude and ambition is always paramount to me when hiring and Haiti was no exception in that regard. A great training program gave these wonderful people a genuine chance. Our trainees had to make it work because there were no options or safety nets if the training failed. Trainees would go their whole life looking for opportunity and they were desperate to make it work. Our trainers were very good at what they did and our trainees learned like their lives depended on it and in many cases it did.

→ We hired 3 full-time trainers. When we were training a class, one trainer taught the class while the other trainers were working with operators on the line. When we were still behind, trainers and even a few bright students became part of the production effort.

→ We believed that training never ends. As our employees got better, their production increased and we could afford to pay production bonuses, which was good for them and the neighbors around the factory. Further, the partners and I loved being able to do better for our employees.

→ Curriculum was enormously important. We basically replicated the 6 week training program that was created by USAID. We recognized that our employees would need specific skills and simply plopping students in front of a sewing machine wasn't going to work.

→ We believed our trainees must be invested in the program. Since they had no money, we didn't charge tuition but we didn't pay them for learning either. We did feed them a hard-boiled egg and a few cookies each day because starving students can't learn.

→ We instructed our trainees to understand what our mission was about and they participated in devotions with the rest of the employees. We also trained them on finances and proper workplace etiquette.

→ Regardless of age, it was the first time most of the students came to a full-time job environment in their lives. We also trained on being on time and staying focused on the job. It helped that we hired employees of aptitude and preached the mission on a nonstop basis.

→ When our trainers hit the production line, we knew that there was going to be a lot of mistakes and we were going to throw out a lot of shirts. We grouped trainees on the same production line and they worked towards making a perfect shirt as a team. It took 6 more weeks after training to gain efficiency.

→ In spite of not having the space or the money, we squeezed a training facility into a corner of the factory and each student had a sewing machine. Since we could only fit 18 machines into a corner, we split the class into morning and afternoon sessions.

The result was that we were able to transform people who had no skills and help them become skilled sewing machine operators in only 6 weeks. Further, they understood how a good employee behaves and why our Economic Mission was so important. When they went to the production line, we supported them with continued training. Because of the support, our new employees were able to reach production numbers that were comparable to the experienced production lines in one month's time. It was thrilling for my partners and me to affordably and efficiently provide these dedicated people with an opportunity of a lifetime. I loved our employees and I was motivated by them. I believe they knew how I felt and therefore management and staff were almost always pushing in the same direction.

The Corporate Set-up

Our Economic Mission is an organization with two business entities. The first entity is a factory that is built with the purpose of delivering aggressive prices and high quality with the objective of competing in the world economy. The second entity is a sales and marketing unit in a developed country that is dedicated to selling everything the factory makes. Angel Investors finance the entire entity by providing interest free and long term loans. Everybody working in the sales and marketing office is considered an Economic Missionary. The subsequent chapters in this book will dive deeper into the topics featured in this chapter.

Why Economic Missions?

An Economic Mission is a complete poverty-reducing vehicle. It sustainably relieves poverty without continual begging. It replaces dependency with dignity. Milton Hershey's factory in Hershey, PA, had a similar effect in the early 1900s. As a mature entity, the Economic Mission can do remarkable things for the surrounding community. Years of payroll being pumped into a community delivers profoundly wonderful results that can change thousands of lives.

The Big Anomaly: Payroll Is an Output, Not an Expense

Since the purpose of the Economic Mission is to pull people out of poverty, and if money is the mechanism that does that, then payroll from the factory is the output that expressly accomplishes the mission goal. Payroll isn't just an output; it is the most important output of the factory. Paying bonuses and spending money on payroll is a wonderful thing. This maximum payroll output mindset changes payroll from an expense to a prosperity-generating output. Increasing payroll and considering it an output is foreign and difficult for any business person to emotionally grasp. When we opened up in Praville, it didn't take long for Fridays and Saturdays to become days when merchants made money because there was $5,000 to $10,000 on the street from payroll. We believe we were the only business in Praville with more than three full-time employees, so when we distribute payroll, everybody lives better. It isn't the work or the profit alone that prevents the community from suffering hunger; it is the payroll that circulates over and over again. In many businesses, payroll is the biggest expense, therefore it is the expense that most business owners try to minimize the most. As a business owner in the US, I always tried to keep payroll in check because payroll was over 80% of my overall expenses. It took at least a year for my heart to catch up with my head and to recognize emotionally how much good a large payday can do in an impoverished community.

Our Pricing Strategy

It's peculiar and we felt unique. Car manufacturers make cars. Bakeries bake breads. Most textile companies make textiles but our textile company saw both polo shirts and elimination of extreme poverty as outputs from our factory. Because of that, our pricing strategy was unique. We were willing to break even or potentially lose a little money on jobs as long as we were earning the slimmest of margins over all. The margin on the shirts we made for the worldwide fast food chain was particularly lean but that was okay because we were able to enhance our "Extreme Poverty Elimination" goal. Since shorter runs didn't significantly drive payroll, we needed to do financially better because that would put us in a position to compete with China and the sweatshops that currently exist today. On large orders from publicly traded companies, we couldn't earn the business based on mission alone. In today's competitive business environment, publicly traded companies seek the best deal so they can remain competitive and maximize profits. It isn't clear if we needed to be the absolute lowest cost provider, but we clearly needed to be very close to the lowest costs. There is also one more product that we make and that will be discussed later in this chapter.

Pravi is "Best Quality" – Here's The Proof

59

About Our Competition

The beautiful thing about our business model is that competitors can understand what we are doing. Competitors can read this book and understand what we did and we will continue to maintain our competitive upper hand. Simply put, our competitors aren't willing to be a mission nor are they willing to give up profits for the sake of their employees. Sweatshop owners don't care about the community that surrounds their factories. Because we care about the long-term health of our employees and communities, we are in a position to accrue extraordinary benefits. It is these benefits that give us our distinct advantage. We will continue to enjoy those advantages as an Economic Mission. And it gets better; as we become better manufacturers, we will continue to be more competitive and we will be in a better position to pay our employees even better. It is essential to reiterate that we are not an NGO and we don't want to use our profits to engage in NGO activities. In Haiti, we did events "for free" for the community but we were determined that those events didn't turn into programs where people expected routine relief.

The Surprise: Vacated Business Expenses

A "Vacated Expense" is an expense that other companies' pay, but due to our Economic Mission status, we can avoid paying. Combined with our ability to generate volume, vacated expenses allow us to favorably compete on price with sweatshops and companies that strive to minimize payroll. Vacated expenses are inherent in the Economic Mission business model. Maximizing the benefits we received from vacating expenses was extremely helpful.

The process of vacating expenses enabled us to pay our employees very well while maintaining price competitiveness in the global market

When attempting to employ hundreds and pull communities out of poverty, driving down costs is critical to growth. Lower costs can dramatically add to the competitive nature of a business. Companies that can reduce costs by $.02 on buttons and $.07 on fabric are the winners of the largest textile contracts. We are constantly finding efficiencies wherever we can. In essence, by cutting costs we are able to pour more money into payroll as long as we stay competitive. Since our competitors are also trying to be efficient, our commitment to growing a large payroll creates an obstacle. It is important to note that for most companies, payroll is their largest expense and controlling payroll is their biggest challenge. If we are undisciplined, our desire to constantly expand payroll can make us uncompetitive. By completely eliminating expenses that virtually all of our competitors have we can pay our employees better and stay competitive. We call these expenses Vacated Expenses.

Thanks to our partners, we were able to acquire a state-of-the-art solar energy network. There were so many panels that we were forced to use the roof of the convent and lunch room. Affordable and consistent energy gave us an advantage and helped us successfully compete in the global market.

Below are some of the areas where we have minimized or eliminated expenses and other cash payments:

Angel Investors: We don't accept donations, but we seek Angel Investors. Because of Angel Investors, we are able to acquire items like buildings, solar energy and high-tech machinery. That saves us from having to pay rent and utilities which makes us more efficient and competitive.

Angel Investors eliminate interest expenses. Angel investors understand that they receive no interest on the principal and that payback would be over an extended period of time. In financial terms, we are not a solid investment because there is not a strong ROI. In terms of virtue, Christian love, and generosity, Angel Investors are making a financial decision that is replete in value and long-term results. Investing in Economic Missions is a no-brainer for people of wealth that have a desire to make this world a better place. If results are important to a potential investor, angel investing in an Economic Mission is wise and prudent.

Angel Investors are attracted to the opportunity of pulling a whole village out of poverty with their investment. A sustainable solution to hopeless poverty is more attractive than getting their money back quickly. An investment that sustainably ends hopeless poverty for thousands of people is a wise investment in mankind and therefore it is very attractive. Because of our Angel Investors, we don't need to adjust our prices so we can hit loan repayment schedules. The Roman philosopher Cicero said, "Virtue is its own reward." It is this virtue that motivates Angel Investors to invest in our Economic Mission. It is about disliking hopeless poverty enough to personally do something about it. For Angel Investors, it is about making a sustainable difference and ending poverty for thousands of people they will probably never meet. It's about making the world a better place.

The capital requirement for the Praville entity was roughly $2.5 million. At 5.5%, interest expense would be about $11,500 per month! The principal payment would require us to generate at least $50,000 in sales per month just to pay the interest. This assumption contradicts the essence of our mission, as it would require us to pay our employees less to meet this expense. Other companies that have these expenses need to adjust their prices upward to cover these costs. We are free to use the savings to increase payroll or lower prices so we can be more competitive.

Utility Payments: In the Third World, electricity is more expensive than in the US. Electricity is generated by big diesel motors that are very costly to operate. The town of Praville didn't have electrical service, and diesel that would run generators was also expensive, so we decided to go with solar energy as our primary source of electricity.

An Angel Investor enabled us to buy a 440-panel system with battery backup and a backup generator. Because the solar energy was free, we saved $5,500 to $6,000 per month. That is almost a week's payroll that we saved each month. To our delight, the system worked remarkably well, and the electricity was void of surges. Without this expense, we are able to price our products even more aggressively or pay our employees even better. Although we had diesel generators, we only used it for backup purposes and we only required it once. Other companies have electricity as a major expense that they need to work into their prices. In Haiti, as fuel became scarce, companies that relied on the electrical grid or their own diesel generators had periods of time when they couldn't operate because of electrical outages. Our total utility expenses were about $100 per month for water and $165 per month for Internet.

Demand for Profits: If the factory owner desires a profit on the bottom line, they need to get it on the top line through sales and higher prices. Our most stringent guiding principle explicitly prohibits anybody with a financial interest from financially profiting in any manner through their efforts in working for or providing services to our Economic Mission. This included board members, the president, Angel Investors etc. Simply put, owners, investors, and partners did not profit from their investment or effort.

In the Spirit of Full Disclosure

Although I say there was no electricity in Praville, that isn't exactly correct. Truth is, Praville had electricity one or 2 days a month. When the convent got electricity, it meant that the bill collectors were coming tomorrow to get paid. The bill collectors would argue that if residents have electricity while we are collecting they should pay for the whole month. Shortly after the sisters paid, the electricity would turn off until it was time to collect for next month. There were no electric meters. They simply made up a number and expected to be paid. When we hooked the convent up to the solar panels, the bill collectors said that the convent should still pay because they are good customers and that is what good customers do. Not dealing with the electricity shysters was also a benefit of having solar power.

In working in the competitive worldwide textile market, I learned that factory owners demand enormous profits for themselves. Many of these competitors have profitability goals that are measured in millions while their employees work for extremely low wages. Textile factory owners driven by greed and enormous profits are particularly vulnerable as they must increase top line prices to secure a strong bottom line profit. When ownership forgoes profits, the vacated expense is saved and empowers the Economic Mission to be more competitive. It isn't unreasonable for the president of the mission to demand the salary of $100,000, which would climb to $130,000 after benefits. When this expense is vacated, a savings of $11,000 per month is accrued. If we are in the position to pay $11,000, we could either give every employee a 30% raise or become more competitive by reducing the cost of our shirts by about $.72. A $.72 per shirt reduction would be an incredibly significant advantage.

Quality Management: Our managers and trainers are Economic Missionaries who believe they are doing the will of God. They have experience in the textile industry and have worked as top executives in the Caribbean's largest factories. They have made the name brands we wear every day. Recruiting management talent in Third World countries is difficult. Managers recognize that opportunity is scarce, and many fear that if the new position doesn't work out, the doors at their old position will be closed. Further, managers have difficulty finding jobs because other managers generally don't leave their jobs. Instead of needing to attract managers with large contracts, we can promote the mission and the will of God. This is more attractive to the type of manager that we want to hire. We saved hundreds of thousands of dollars by not having to recruit managers from out of the country and offering big salaries. Besides the financial advantage, our managers see the development of our employees as a critical step in doing God's will. Many of our managers are motivated by mission over money. We get better quality because our trainers feel good about training and our employees are grateful for the opportunity to learn. Although we can't quantify the savings, I believe we are saving at least $10,000 per month by recruiting with our mission instead of offering bigger salaries.

HOPE Act: In Haiti, we qualified for tariff relief under the HOPE Act, which allowed us to ship things to and from the United States without paying tariffs. The HOPE Act was put in place to help deeply impoverished countries compete in the world market against suppliers that have large-scale operation benefits. Although this isn't a result of us being an Economic Mission, it does allow us to compete more effectively in the world market. We believe the tariff rate is 16.5% for our type of product. The estimated savings is sizable. Since we are competing with countries that also benefit from the HOPE Act, it is not an exclusive benefit of an Economic Mission. It is important to recognize, however, that China and other countries in the Asian Pacific Rim don't have these benefits, and the HOPE Act is an advantage in most instances.

Other Benefits: As an Economic Mission, we received other financial benefits. A precise valuation of these benefits is difficult. For example, we don't pay rent, but that is because an Angel Investor paid for the construction of our building and we have a 0% mortgage. Having our building built on these terms is a blessing, but the exact amount of the savings is somewhat ambiguous. Weber Advertising, the marketing firm that I sold to partners, is allowing me to set up my US sales entity in their offices rent free. Weber Advertising has also built websites, provided technology and printing for us. Without a doubt, they are the best supporters who have never stroked a check. Like Angel Investors, these people want to see entire villages pulled out of poverty and they are along for the ride. They aren't investing, but their generous offer saves thousands on a monthly basis. Even my Sunday school class and parishioners at Saint Joseph Church in Lancaster, PA, have volunteered professional services to help me be successful. The services could be valued at thousands of dollars annually, and when I get them at no cost; it helps me to be competitive in the world market.

In summary, we were saving at least $50,000 per month through our vacated expenses. This was why we could be price competitive in the world market. In fact, in our first year of operation, the money we saved from vacated expenses surpassed the amount of money we paid in payroll. We enjoy these benefits because we are an Economic Mission. If we didn't have Angel Investors or Vacated Expenses, we would be hemorrhaging cash as a startup and there would be pressure to get profitable very quickly. As we grow, our employees and the people who surround our factory will benefit because the cost per shirt will decrease. As we grow, our customers will also benefit because we will be able to be the low-cost provider. Unlike other companies, maximizing profits isn't an objective so we can gain long-term high dollar relationships. Further, companies can feel good about our factory.

These cost reductions allowed our relatively small production facility to successfully compete in the global market. We are able to buy the necessary supplies, manufacture the shirt, and ship it to the US for less than $4.75 per polo shirt. Of that $4.75, $1.50 per shirt was allocated to employee payroll. At a production level of 275,000 shirts, we could budget $412,000 per year for payroll, or about $7500 per week for after-tax payroll. Our annual payroll was within 5% of that number. We spent slightly less than $3 on cost of goods sold and transportation. We didn't need large net sales because we had vacated expenses. As we grew, we were able to further reduce our labor costs on a per shirt basis. We expected the per shirt labor cost to further diminish as production increased. With four or five production lines, we could manufacture and deliver shirts for $4.10 per shirt. Our minimum costs could be less if we used cheaper materials, but we want to maintain a standard of quality. It is entirely conceivable, and even likely, that we could one day have the lowest US landed costs for polo shirts in the world.

The net result is that we can compete with anybody based on quality and price. As evidence of our competitiveness, we landed major contracts with a fortune 500 uniform supplier and an international fast food franchise. This was in our first year of operation, and our processes were not close to being refined. These companies are sensitive to price and quality. Our Vacated Expenses Business Model, in conjunction with our mission, helped make our clients' decision to buy from us easier.

An Economic Mission Is a Business

Like any business, we need to make a profit, even if that profit is small. We still need to pay back Angel Investors and reinvest in our company by buying equipment that can make us more efficient. Like any business, we need to be improving every day, and we practice business principles like Kaizen. Using the continued improvement methods of Kaizen, we need to be committed to efficiently making our products and systems better. Our success teeters on the quality of our work; therefore our employees must be trained. Like any other business, if employees can't do the job, they must be replaced. We had a wonderful maintenance worker who contributed greatly to the factory. He was good at what he did except he had difficulty working on small things like sewing machines, so we had to let him go. This was particularly hard because we liked him and we knew that it was going to be a long time before he gets another job. That is what a business would do.

We have a deeply held belief that excellence and Christian standards can coexist in our mission. Further, our Christian standards thrive when we expect more from ourselves. We demand that our employees be on time and that they be productive. Except for 11:45 AM daily devotions and the Christian music that often plays during work hours, neighbors might not even know that we are a Christian Economic Mission. Acting like a business isn't a license for us to be uncaring or egotistical. We need to remember that we are called to do something that hasn't been done before. We are doing the will of God, and that includes making our business stronger and more competitive because strength is what will provide sustainability of this model into the future.

An Economic Mission Is a Christian Mission

As a mission, we can never forget that we are there for a very specific mission: to pull the community that surrounds our factory out of hopeless poverty. At the same time, we need to build a Christian culture that draws each person more closely to Jesus. We are also making disciples. The list of what we manufacture increases again. We produce high quality polo shirts, extreme poverty relief and now disciples. It's a great business model! We need to be loyal to our mission, and we need to accomplish that mission. As a Christian mission, we must continue to keep God in the center of our lives. It is our responsibility to consistently provide an atmosphere where our employees can draw near to God on a daily and even hourly basis. As we engage with the community, it is essential that our neighbors know our distinct Christian identity. We are doing the will of God and we must manage this operation in a way that brings people closer to God.

Being a Christian mission doesn't imply that we are soft or weak. We must be sure that we maintain expectations but, at the same time, achieve results. Our Economic Mission is committed to achieving financial success, which is why our mission has a different feel about it. Christian ethics and a determination to succeed must simultaneously coexist. We can never let quality slide, and we must demand the best from every employee. Maintaining price and quality competitiveness is what makes us a good business. Guiding our workers to Christ and assisting our staff in growing as better Christians is what defines us as a good Christian Economic Mission.

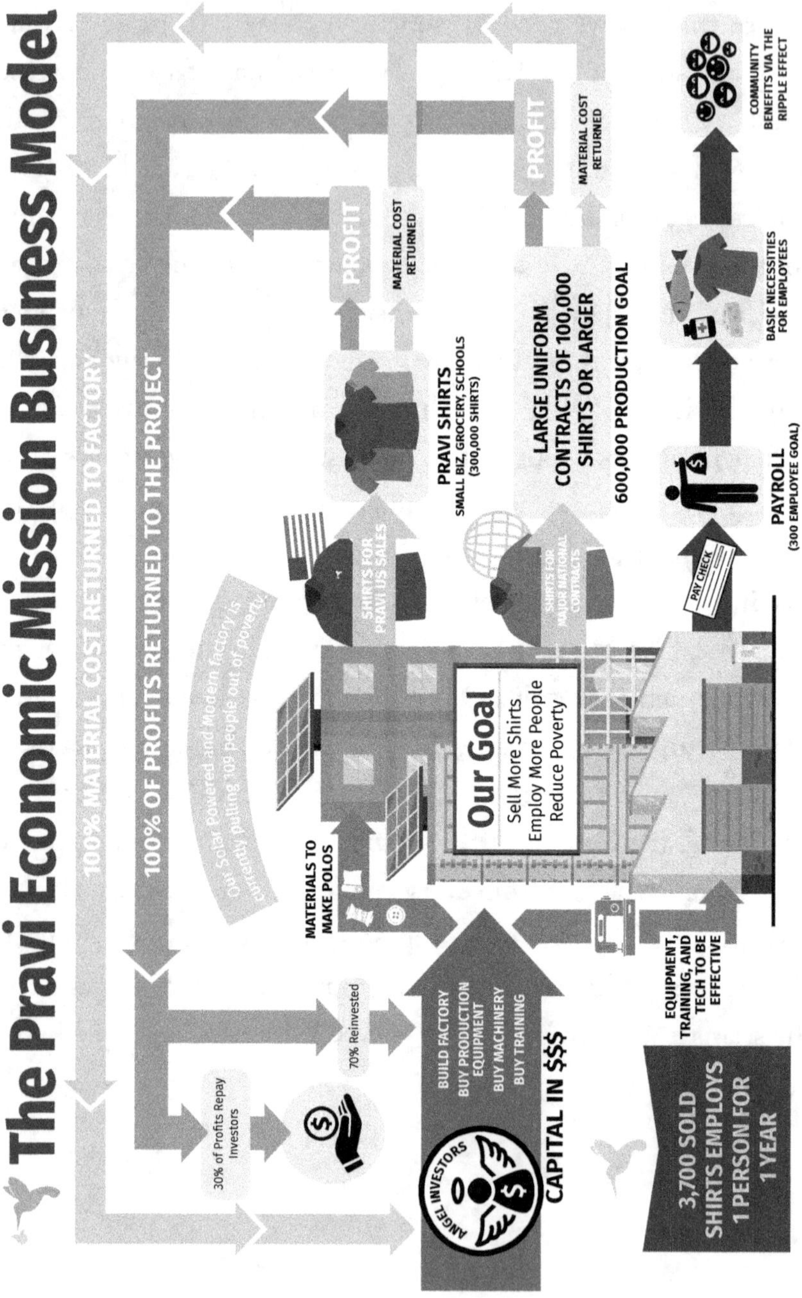
The Pravi Economic Mission Business Model
100% MATERIAL COST RETURNED TO FACTORY
100% OF PROFITS RETURNED TO THE PROJECT
30% of Profits Repay Investors
70% Reinvested
ANGEL INVESTORS
BUILD FACTORY
BUY PRODUCTION EQUIPMENT
BUY MACHINERY
BUY TRAINING
CAPITAL IN $$$
MATERIALS TO MAKE POLOS
Our Solar Powered and Modern factory is currently putting 109 people out of poverty.
Our Goal
Sell More Shirts
Employ More People
Reduce Poverty
SHIRTS FOR PRAVI US SALES
SHIRTS FOR MAJOR NATIONAL CONTRACTS
PRAVI SHIRTS
SMALL BIZ, GROCERY, SCHOOLS (300,000 SHIRTS)
LARGE UNIFORM CONTRACTS OF 100,000 SHIRTS OR LARGER
600,000 PRODUCTION GOAL
PROFIT
MATERIAL COST RETURNED
PROFIT
MATERIAL COST RETURNED
EQUIPMENT, TRAINING, AND TECH TO BE EFFECTIVE
PAY CHECK
PAYROLL
(300 EMPLOYEE GOAL)
BASIC NECESSITIES FOR EMPLOYEES
COMMUNITY BENEFITS VIA THE RIPPLE EFFECT
3,700 SOLD SHIRTS EMPLOYS 1 PERSON FOR 1 YEAR

4 - THE ECONOMIC MISSION DIFFERENCE

*It is how 104 employees made life
better for thousands of people.*

There is a difference between relieving hunger and ending hopeless poverty. It is important to remember that we are talking about "extreme poverty," which we are also calling "hopeless poverty." The goal of the Economic Mission is to eliminate hunger, homelessness, and hopelessness and improve the lives of the people that surround it. We recognize that nobody will get rich because of our Economic Mission, but hopeless poverty will be eliminated for our employees and greatly diminished for our neighbors who live near our factory.

Of course, employees of Economic Missions are the biggest winners. Generally, they are able to feed themselves, keep themselves in better clothing, keep their homes maintained, and even add rooms to what was once a single-room house. In our factory in Haiti, very few of our employees owned a refrigerator or even a bicycle. Lives were vastly improved; our employees were eating proteins and benefiting from healthier diets. Employees were also eating multiple meals each day. Most employees lived with 7 or 8 family members and they were also able to keep them healthy. Their children could attend school and owned shoes. These might seem like low standards, but it is a giant step up from malnutrition, starvation, and hopeless poverty.

The Payroll Ripple Effect

The degree of success that our mission attains depends on our ability to bolster the payroll dollars that our employees receive. Higher degrees of success can be accomplished by either paying employees more or by increasing production, therefore requiring more employees. By expanding payroll, more money circulates in the community, which can be earned by those not directly employed by the Economic Mission. Every Friday, our employees receive their pay. As a result, every Friday evening and Saturday, the impact of the payroll ripples through the streets. A one dollar bill will leave an employee's hand and move into the hands of someone who is poor. Because the person who received the dollar is in great need, it moves quickly to someone else. That dollar could move to 6, 8 or even 10 hands in a single day. Best of all, with every hand a dollar touches, it helps to alleviate hopeless poverty and hunger. By being in a densely populated area, these dollars are turned more frequently since the ripple effect isn't slowed down by transportation issues. Each Friday a new wave of payroll dollars causes this life-improving ripple effect. In contrast, the dollar invested in a feeding program would only get used once, and that isn't as effective. The goal for our Economic Mission is to drive a large payroll without losing money.

In the community surrounding the factory, conditions improved for the vendors and citizens. Each Friday, a wave of about $8000 flowed into the community, and that was a great benefit for our neighbors. People who sold shoes, food, clothing, water and all kinds of items were doing better. A thirty percent increase in banana sales meant that the banana salesperson could spend more money on things they needed and wanted. New markets for items like aspirin, personal hygiene products, and even solar powered lights emerged. Because the majority of items were purchased locally, the factory payroll circulated repeatedly within a small radius of the factory. It was wonderful to see what regular payroll did to the local economy. As things got better, hopeless poverty turned into hope, and even people who weren't employees lived better.

The Birthday Party

After being in business for one year, I learned that a six-year-old resident of Praville had a birthday party, and there was a cake and even a small birthday present. It meant a lot for me and my partners because that meant that we were making a difference. There were hundreds of stories like birthday parties, kids getting shoes, kids going to school, and families enjoying multiple daily meals that made it clear that our model was working. Nobody got rich, but life got better and there was continuing improvement. The kids looked healthier and people were making money by selling goods and services in the expanding local economy.

The Chick-Fil-A of Praville, Haiti

As the factory began operations, individuals not employed also capitalized on the opportunities that arose. In the first week after our first payday, I met Shedlene as she began selling snacks and other items for lunch. Her children had all of the telltale signs of malnutrition. She continually reinvested in her business and in her family. In 6 weeks, I returned to see Shedlene  offering a variety of lunch specials and her children were in clean clothes and healthier. She had bigger pans and I could see that she was implementing systems that made her more efficient. She was a committed businesswoman who made sure everybody was happy and that the line kept moving. She was always there and smiling. Our employees could depend on her and, of course, the employees enjoyed her cooking. She is quite possibly the best success story we had and I didn't pay her or control her in any way. She was guided by the desire to succeed and she did it in a loving way. She became the Chik-fil-A of Praville, Haiti!

Regarding Effectiveness

Generosity has degrees of effectiveness. Something as simple as handing a couple dollars out of a car window to a homeless person can be misused. Even that simple act of love can be very ineffective. In my personal efforts to assist former prisoners and homeless individuals, I need to adopt a comprehensive approach, justifying failures by the results achieved when a plan eventually works. This mentality has been referred to as the leaking bucket principle. Although the system is inefficient, like a leaking bucket, it is better than having no system or bucket. When we accept these "leaking buckets" as comprehensive solutions, we end up adopting stagnant and ineffective strategies for the long term. When loaning impoverished persons money to get back on their feet, seeing that effort fail hurts. It isn't just about getting repaid. The failure, which mostly rests with the people that were being helped, leaves the borrower wondering about what could have been. Generally speaking, our culture has accepted the leaking bucket of hunger relief. Phrases such as "Haiti Fatigue" have been coined to describe the sense of hopelessness donors experience when their consistent contributions to Haiti don't seem to create any substantial change. Wasted effort is very demoralizing.

Adam Smith pointed out in The Theory of Moral Sentiments that we are intrinsically driven to do what's right. The payoff is a feeling of goodness. He argued that goodness is driven by human emotions. Unfortunately, these emotions can be frequently satisfied via a leaky bucket. Although this previous statement generalizes a great philosophy, it is safe to say that we all hate to fail, and that includes when we try to help our fellow citizens. The Economic Mission concept is about making it personal and being driven to absolutely succeed.

Eliminate the Root Causes Instead of Symptoms

The hallmark of the Economic Mission lies in the diminishing of the root causes of extreme poverty. We live in a world of quick fixes, but too often those solutions cover up symptoms instead of treating the root causes. In other words, the problem is still there. Our world covers up symptoms instead of generating solutions. Doctors push high blood pressure medicine because they don't want to tell their patients to lose weight. We give kids seventh place soccer trophies so they can feel good about themselves without working hard. Advertising people convince millions of misguided consumers that they deserve a better life and that a new car that isn't affordable is the key to that better life. We rarely address the root problem. In today's society, it might be considered rude to tell people to spend less; instead, we tell them to negotiate down their credit card balances and that their inability to live a disciplined life isn't their fault. The reality is that everything isn't quick, easy or free.

The quick fix culture is also having an effect on how we help our fellow human beings and it isn't good. It doesn't even have to be effective or efficient as long as we can tell ourselves that we did something. We have lost some of the moral sentiments that Adam Smith was talking about in 1759. When people are hungry and personally failing, we no longer help them or counsel them. In some circles, counseling is considered politically incorrect. Instead, we point them to an organization that will cover up the symptom, and we fool ourselves into feeling good for making that suggestion. I believe millions of Americans believe that they truly care for the poor by saying that the government should be doing more for poor people and that the government should be taxing other people to pay for it. To me, it seems very hypocritical. Our culture allows us to care less and quick fixes are part of that culture. Quick fixes, even if they aren't successful, provide us with a nice way to check the box. Quick fixes allow us to feel good in spite of making no real difference. Once we check the box, we are free to continue to focus on self.

Fixing our problem of self and their problem of poverty takes more time and caring than a quick fix that simply offers a good feeling. The problem is that symptom cover-ups aren't permanent or even efficient. A broken culture is what is left when symptoms are addressed instead of solving root problems. Since the root problems don't go away, we will spend time and money for years covering the symptoms of poverty. As new people have new problems, we will simply add to the need. By demanding that somebody else does more, we fool ourselves into believing that we are doing good without really helping or caring. It is a vicious cycle. By blaming businesses, governments, or rich people, we are further able to cover our own personal symptom of self-centeredness.

Economic Missions offer sustainable, long-term results. "Fix it right the first time" is the attitude that drives the success of the Economic Mission. In the areas where we go, the root cause of poverty is a lack of opportunity. The solution isn't a robust feeding program. The solution for permanent change in the Third World is to make a sustainable difference by creating opportunity.

DIFFERENT PHILOSOPHIES FOR HELPING THE POOR

CHARITY THINKING...

"Feed the world, let them know it's Christmas time."

- Band Aid

EMPOWERING THINKING...

"Give a man a fish and you feed him for a day; teach a man to fish and you feed him for a lifetime."

- Maimonides – Ancient Philosopher

ECONOMIC MISSION THINKING...

"Teach a man to fish and you feed him for a lifetime, give a man the opportunity export fish and he will also improve life for the whole community, and best of all, he can occasionally enjoy a cheeseburger instead of eating fish every single day."

- Jim Weber

Opportunity Is Hard Work

Creating opportunity instead of covering up symptoms requires a deeper level of commitment. It requires caring individuals to slow down and ask the right questions. It also requires organizations to listen. Finding opportunity requires creative thinking and dedicated doers. In his book, The Obstacle Is the Way, Ryan Holiday explains that ancient Stoic philosophy shows us how the obstacles aren't in the way but instead that clearing the obstacle actually becomes the way. Instead of treating symptoms, we need to clear obstacles that impoverish. Clearing impoverishing obstacles is permanent, while covering up symptoms requires constant attention. When the solution is permanent, it sustains itself and there is little or no burden in the future.

The biggest benefit the Economic Mission offers is permanence. Covering up symptoms requires ongoing attention and expense. By providing opportunities instead of rice packets, we are improving the lives of our employees and their community on a long-term basis. A permanent solution, like clearing impoverishing obstacles, is liberating. Treating a symptom by having people beg for food is enslaving and demeaning. When impoverishing obstacles can be cleared, it should be. When obstacles can be cleared, symptom relief is required, and that will be unfortunate and expensive for a long time to come.

Yetta was living with her children on less than $3 per day. While working her other job, she participated in our training program and became a wonderful employee. Her income went up by 500% when she began working at the factory. She wasn't getting rich, but Yetta and her children were no longer starving. She was actively participating in devotions and also became more spiritual.

Long Term Effects of Covering Symptoms

In Haiti, symptoms are covered up by well-meaning NGO/nonprofit organizations and their donors. The root causes are never addressed. There are shipping lines with multiple ships that are dedicated to bringing food into Haiti by the container load. Countries pour billions of dollars into Haiti, yet there is still widespread hunger and poverty. Haiti's largest import is humanitarian aid. As a country, Haiti's best skill lies in their ability to position themselves as victims so they can receive more aid. The people and the government have become addicted to begging. It is sad to see people waiting for the Haitian government to take care of them when the government is so weak they can't even keep the red light in the town square working. This is a by-product of covering up the symptoms of poverty over multiple generations. Citizens expect the Haitian government to protect them and their family, while the reality is that the people need to protect themselves from the government.

To demonstrate, let's compare Japan in 1945 to Haiti in 2010. After nuclear bombs were dropped in Japan and after the 2010 Haitian earthquake, massive amounts of relief funds poured into those countries. It was reported that $13.5 billion was pumped into Haiti. The vast majority of that $13.5 billion was wasted. After World War II obliterated Japan, the United States provided aid in the amount of $1.9 billion, or $26 per person. Adjusted for inflation, that amount would be $430. With that money, Japan solved the root causes of their poverty by building factories. They became strong in the world market and could take care of themselves. After the earthquake, Haiti received $1,220 per capita which is 285% more money on a per person basis when adjusted for inflation. The amount was approximately equal to the average annual income. The Haitian culture permitted and even promoted failure. Haiti went back to begging. The commitment to addressing symptoms instead of combating root causes is a major reason why Haiti still begs today. Symptom cover-up is the reason Haiti's largest import is humanitarian aid.

Opportunity Changes Everything

If we want things to change in the hopelessly poor parts of the world, we need to provide opportunity. The factory in Praville and Economic Missions in general were great opportunities for people and communities to pull themselves out of poverty. Our employees took full advantage and made the most of their opportunity. At the factory, our attendance is over 99.5%, and our on-time rate is equally impressive. Even though our employees get paid on a daily rate, many of them stay late so they can hit the established daily goals. When people have opportunity, the human spirit drives them to do great things. Our employees are making bonuses, and they love that their success means we are hiring more people. When people get an opportunity, they do amazing things.

SIDE STORY

The Desire for Opportunity

In Haiti, earthquakes are particularly frightening. The 2010 earthquake in Haiti was horrific. Over 11% of the population of Port-au-Prince and 2 ½% of the entire population of Haiti died. In August 2021, I was doing interviews when a 7.2 earthquake struck. Although the earthquake was much weaker in Praville, it immediately brought back the fears from 2010. As I saw employees and candidates react, I decided to pause interviews. Upon hearing about the delay, and thinking that the interviews would be canceled, the candidates insisted on continuing the interview process, in spite of their concerns about a bigger earthquake following. They were willing to risk their own well-being for the opportunity to get a job.

The Difference Between 501(c)(3) charities and Economic Missions

Both 501(c)(3) charities and Economic Missions are managed by service-driven people that want to make a difference in a wonderful way. Another similarity is that neither charities nor Economic Missions can totally eliminate poverty or hunger throughout the world. Finally, neither organization offers a complete "set it and forget it" scenario. Charities have the work of constantly raising money. The Economic Mission has to get their products to the US as they are ordered so they can be sold. Both of these tasks are sizable.

The biggest difference between an Economic Mission and a 501(c)(3) charity is one of permanence. Most charities have a broad base of people for whom they supply temporary relief. These organizations provide food, medicine, and other necessities to keep the poorest of the poor alive. Some initiatives are more permanent, like well drilling. While 501(c)(3) organizations are characterized by always asking for money and always being in need, an Economic Mission is an entity that is dedicated to eliminating hopeless poverty by using commerce and job creation as tools. There is no institutional begging with the Economic Mission business model. Building and operating a factory in an impoverished area changes everything. The employees benefit most, but as money is pumped into the community via payroll, the merchants do better, locals hire, and jobs are created, thus the general population lives better. Like the 501(c)(3), funds were solicited, but it was for capital to build the mission. Unlike the 501(c)(3), that community won't have a lingering fiscal need, and therefore, we don't need to constantly ask for money.

Another difference is that charitable organizations are middlemen. That said, middlemen get a bad rap. When we want butter, bread, and oranges, we go to the grocery store, which is a middleman. The grocer has marked up the price and therefore takes his cut, and, of course, there is an elevated price. Although we would rather pay the lower price, we enjoy the convenience more than saving a few dollars. In essence, we are paying the middleman for making charitable actions easier for us. This also holds true for many 501(c)(3) organizations. When sending donations, percentages are taken out for salaries, marketing, rent, and other overhead costs. Many of these costs are significant so donations are less effective. In an Economic Mission, every dollar goes to the business model that best pulls people out of poverty. Every dollar has a clear mission: to pull people out of poverty. Just like the payroll dollar being spent multiple times, the investment in an Economic Mission works every day to pull communities out of hopeless poverty.

It is important to note that middlemen may choose to raise their margin and increase their profitability whenever they can. Charitable organizations are no different and they will raise the amount that stays "in house". It is well documented that NGO and Civil Servant salaries continue to climb. Over time, employees of charitable organizations see themselves as the charity and the comfort of the organization becomes more important than the people who were once the benefactors of the organization. This may be in part, the fault of the donor who blindly throws enormous amounts of money without demanding value accountability. In Haiti, multitudes of NGOs have manipulated donors and taken more than a middleman's share. If donations are unspecific in nature, NGOs can and will do anything they desire and that includes overhead increases. Worse yet, your donation can be fraudulently taken without supplying any benefit to the poorest of the poor. This happens far too often in Haiti and other third world countries.

Providing food, clothing, water, and even healthcare for the poorest of the poor is certainly virtuous. Jennifer and I founded "The Cookie Sale to Combat World Hunger," which is a hunger relief effort. For over twenty-five years, we have been providing millions of meals annually for people who would otherwise go hungry. The proceeds from our sale feed about ten thousand people each day. These efforts don't eliminate poverty, and if we don't or someone else doesn't feed these people, they will starve. We aren't combating poverty, and we aren't attacking the root cause of that poverty. In Matthew 25, Christ clearly points out that we are responsible to take care of the hungry and the poor. The reality is that there will always be poor people, and therefore we will always need organizations that can provide the most basic necessities for the poorest of the poor. Charitable organizations make it possible for us to do good things on three separate continents without missing a day of work. For that service, we pay a markup to charitable organizations.

The Economic Mission is different in Third World communities. It attacks the significant root cause of poverty and provides opportunity. The Economic Mission provides opportunities for people to build their own lives and pull themselves out of poverty. The Economic Mission also provides the training that enables our employees to take advantage of the opportunity. We often say that our employees work like their lives depend on it. The people who do not work in the factory also recognize opportunity. As payroll ripples through the streets, locals also enjoy opportunity as it arises.

According to Brookings and the World Bank, it is estimated that 648 million people are living on less than $2.15 per day (2017 dollars, PPP Basis). That is an unimaginable amount of violent desperation. Charitable relief organizations can provide relief to more of them than a system of Economic Missions can. However, charitable relief organizations can do virtually nothing to alter that course for these people. An Economic Mission can reduce the number of hopelessly impoverished people. The Economic Mission needs the right conditions to be successful. For example, the Economic Mission works best in densely populated areas. That precludes helping a significant portion of the world's poor, who live in rural conditions. The Economic Mission provides opportunity, but if a lack of opportunity isn't the source of poverty, the Economic Mission will not be effective. Economic Missions are not a one size fits all solution for worldwide poverty. However, if opportunity is the obstacle, Economic Missions deliver better results.

Another key difference is that donors donate to poverty-focused charities, while investors invest in Economic Missions. Naturally, an investment in an Economic Mission isn't necessarily an investment in the classic sense of the word because it isn't about risk and reward. An interest-free loan will be worth less when the money is returned than it was when it was invested. The profit that comes from an investment in an Economic Mission is emotional and in the heart. An investor knows that their investment isn't typical, but it is worth the effort knowing that their investment will save an entire community from hopelessness. In a world where some people have everything they want, this kind of investment fulfills a personal need for an investor to become the best version of themselves.

Working in an Economic Mission, we hear that providing sustainable jobs is teaching people to fish instead of feeding people fish. It is cliché, and I often respond that we do even better than that. We teach people to export and thrive. It is the goal of the Economic Mission that as people build skills, they build sustainable independence. They build for themselves a sense of dignity that handouts can never offer. When successful, the Economic Mission allows charitable organizations to focus on other impoverished communities. The goal of the Economic Mission is to reduce the number of people that need to be "taken care of." The Economic Mission can move people from dependence to dignity.

We look forward to the day when we have multiple Economic Missions and each mission is paid off. It could be our goal to have some type of employee ownership. Since the factory and the United States sales unit are dependent on each other, this would create issues that need to be addressed. At that time, we will need to decide how to let the labor force and the local management receive an ownership interest while guaranteeing our mission objectives into the future.

The Difference Between the Mission Trip and the Economic Mission

At first glance, it might appear that the mission trip and the Economic Mission are very similar. In reality, the differences are quite stark. Economic Missions are about opportunity, while mission trips build empathy for those who are poor. In reality, mission trips often diminish opportunity for people in poor communities to succeed. Before I did work in Haiti, I thought mission trips were a wonderful way to reach out to those less fortunate countries. While working in Haiti, I learned how mission trips can hurt a community. Economics is the study of scarcity and in poor countries work and opportunity are very scarce. The economics of that situation clearly indicate that by doing the local carpenter's job his opportunity to earn a living is being eliminated. As mission trip participants perform tasks, they are taking jobs from local tradesmen. With money raised from car washes and bake sales, well-meaning people build schools, churches, and homes that could have been built by local tradesmen. This eliminates the opportunity for the local craftsmen to do their jobs which fosters poverty. The rule is simple: In a Third World country, never do anything that a local person can do, because that is eliminating opportunity for local people.

In the book, When Helping Hurts, the authors promote asset-based community development and encourage readers to focus on the resources and abilities that the community has to empower people. At the factory in Praville, there was a sense of pride that couldn't be replaced by a handout.

Imagine this: Suppose thirty-four kids and eleven chaperones from Slidell, Louisiana go to Jamaica to build a school in a poor community for ten days. At $600 per person for airfare, taxes, transportation to the airport, passports, and maybe even new luggage, $27,000 would be spent before they even arrived in Jamaica. An additional $40 per person per night for lodging is another $16,200. This doesn't take into consideration that the chaperones have opportunity costs that accrue from missing work. After spending $43,000, they go to some remote community and begin building the school.

At Least Nobody Lost Their Job

There is a school between Ennery and Cap Haitien where the principal would chuckle and say their classrooms are getting smaller every year. Apparently, a mission group would come to the school and paint the walls on an annual basis whether it was needed or not. They would also bring a cash donation for the school. The only way the school could get the cash donation was to let the mission group paint the walls of the school. Locally, the running joke was that there was so much paint on the walls that the classrooms were actually growing smaller because of all of the coats of paint. The silver lining here is that even though the school didn't need paint, this mission trip didn't take anybody's job, because the walls weren't going to get painted anyway. From one perspective, if the cost of the trip had been added to the cash donation, a school feeding program could have been implemented. From another perspective, there is wisdom in having students work with the poor and for the poor without taking anybody's job. In the 2nd perspective, American students learned life lessons and workers in Haiti didn't get hurt. That's kind of clever!

The hungry Jamaican carpenter that is looking for work has lost that opportunity to build the school. A well-meaning Christian cheerleader from Slidell and her fun-loving friends have taken the opportunity for a Jamaican carpenter to feed his family. Their act of love and all of their effort eliminates the demand for local workers as they lose those opportunities to build those houses. The better course would be to send two envoys with $40,000 to hire local carpenters and pay for the supplies to get houses built. The envoys would pay locals to polish the rented car, do their laundry, carry bags to the room, and any other task they can create to spend money. The envoys would also make sure the construction job was done perfectly and without fraud.

As churches and groups organize mission trips, they need to be cognizant of the jobs they could be eliminating as they perform tasks that locals do. If mission participants are holding a hammer or a paintbrush, they are taking an opportunity from a local crafts-man. If a mission trip participant is doing something on their trip that could be done by a local person, they are taking a local's opportunity. The mission trip can actually cause poverty on a micro level by diminishing opportunity.

Undoubtedly, a mission trip after a major hurricane is a wonderful thing because these areas immediately need as much help as possible. If churches and organizations want to have their young members working, they could tentatively set aside a week in mid-August. As happens every year, a hurricane or earthquake will significantly damage a Caribbean island. At that time, hammer-swinging and paintbrush-wielding missionaries can do their work without diminishing opportunities. Also, if a church desires to send a group to teach the gospel, that is a good thing as well. Spreading the gospel is providing opportunity to the highest degree. Sending doctors to an area where there is no medical help is a wonderful thing too.

When done correctly, a mission trip can help a student understand in their heart that not everybody lives as well as they do. Surely this pays future dividends as people become sensitive to poverty issues. This could be accomplished without leaving the country, and the savings from airline tickets can be used to fund community enhancement in those areas. This frugal generosity that is being learned could also pay future dividends. If leaving the country is preferred, a more educational approach could have lasting results. A mission group could visit extremely poor communities and hand out food or they could visit any Third World landfill where they can see kids picking through rotting garbage and fighting rats for food. They can feed those kids and learn wonderful lessons at the same time.

Micro-Finance Is Awesome

I love micro-finance. The goal of micro-finance is to help make an impoverished entrepreneur self-sufficient by offering low-interest loans. Some micro-finance efforts will help people buy cows, and their owners live off the milk that is sold and eventually pay off the debt. I was reading about one micro-finance investment where a poor entrepreneur got into business making wheelbarrows for an investment of a couple hundred bucks. Years later he even had employees. Micro-finance is about dignity and freedom. It is a wonderful thing.

As a promoter of Economic Missions, I am a little envious of micro-financing organizations and the freedom people have to become the best versions of themselves. As an Economic Mission, we provide opportunity, but we don't build entrepreneurs. On the other hand, micro-financing only helps the surrounding community in very small ways. Unlike micro-finance, the Economic Mission has the power to put thousands of dollars on the streets week after week. Further, Economic Missions have a security about them. A steady paycheck ensures they will always have food on their tables. During hurricanes and earthquakes, the employees of the Economic Mission know that they will be going back to work soon. The difference is that while micro-finance pulls a family out of poverty, an Economic Mission aspires to pull an entire community out of poverty. In both instances, when successful, nobody gets rich, but people get above poverty lines with dignity.

As we grow, our Economic Mission can turn to micro-finance as a way to keep payroll local. By adding additional local goods and services, payroll would "stay home" longer. Further, the profits from the Micro-financed business would add to the local economy and those profits would get spent over and over again.

More Than Hunger

My experiences have shown me that just beyond the pains of hunger and violent desperation was a person who was suffering. They are often also emotionally scarred. Their battle to survive is far more desperate and even animalistic than we perceive. The photo of the poor family doesn't tell the whole story. They have beaten up people and have been beaten up for a piece of bread. Some have prostituted their own children because if they didn't, they would starve. There is a violence that comes with hopeless poverty, and the photograph doesn't tell the whole story. We must not forget they are God's children that have been put into a living hell. We can't undo those scars, but we can let them see that we have compassion in our hearts. I learned to never treat people like victims because victims never thrive. I learned that a smile, a joke, or even playing soccer with locals may briefly alleviate the pain of poverty but not the pain of hunger. When someone is hungry in the Third World sense, nothing but food can improve that situation. Diminished hunger through payroll was our first success in Praville. I like talking with neighbors around the factory. I will never create jobs fast enough, but I hope that locals know I am trying. For our employees, we made sure they knew when they did a great job and that they were the source of our desire to add more jobs. A little bit of beer and loud music after work on a Friday made payday even better. I love my employees and the neighbors that I got to know. My life is better because of them.

Our employees genuinely cared for each other and formed lifelong friendships. The miracle in Praville helped them become family instead of coworkers.

"Luck is a dividend of sweat. The more you sweat the luckier you get."
Ray Kroc

5 - AMOR FATI: ACCEPTING FATE

Working on an Economic Mission is painfully wonderful.

My perception of mission work was much different before I started my Economic Mission than it is now. I expected the highs and even the lows, but I didn't expect the low times to be so low. To survive, I adopted a Stoic philosophy of amor fati, which literally means to "love your fate." Although I can't "love" the bad things that happened to me as an Economic Missionary, I can see how they made me stronger. I can appreciate the path that I am on. I constantly remind myself that what I am doing is difficult and I will never be comfortable. To me, amor fati means acceptance, instead of loving the bad things. By accepting and even expecting bad things to happen, I can be better prepared for the big challenges when they happen. I have tried to understand what life is like in a Third World country with a crooked government. It would be foolish to expect anything but difficulty. By controlling expectations, I am mentally prepared for all of the difficulties that tomorrow will bring. It helps me recognize that I can't control many things that are happening to me in my life, but I can control how I let those things affect me.

Just Another Extortion Story

The US government granted companies in Haiti tariff free status through the HOPE Act. Unfortunately, I had to work with the Haitian CFI office to get "a franchise" which allows me tariff free status. It was the job of the CFI to attract businesses to Haiti and a large part of their job was to convince me that Haiti is not corrupt. As I filed the paperwork, I received a call from my attorney saying that the CFI was demanding $50,000 which would be split up between decision-makers or they wouldn't approve my franchise. After presenting them with correspondence from my Congressman and informing them that I had a friend who worked for the TV show 60 Minutes, they finally backed off their request. However, the 20 day process took over 2 years and we are still not sure if we ever had our franchise.

The Ugly Side of Mission Work

Mission work is far more difficult than I would have ever thought. I learned quickly that if I want to pull people out of poverty, there are a multitude of unfortunate situations and obstacles that I will need to overcome. I was extorted, had my life threatened, was a victim of theft, and was cheated more times than I can count. I even had an employee potentially set me up to be kidnapped. Most Haitians see me as the rich white guy, and I was a target to be cheated. I never felt safe, and there were plenty of reasons for that.

This is what remains of our $47,000 automated placket machine which was our biggest investment on the production line. They also destroyed the generator, industrial air compressor and other equipment that was too heavy to move.

In the time I spent in Haiti, I learned to expect anything. Before the factory was destroyed, I recognized that a politician or drug dealer might do something horrible to our factory. We saw it as unlikely because so many people were benefiting in Praville. We weren't completely surprised that an AK-47 armed mob attacked our factory, but I was disheartened to see the number of locals raiding our factory after they left. We better understand the culture of ignorance and we recognize that we must do business differently. If the Economic Mission ever grows to its full potential and if there are multiple factories in the world, it is logical for me to expect additional attacks. That is the ugly reality that would accompany success. Amor Fati!

I need to take the good with the bad. As I do the will of God, I have an audience of one that I am trying to please. I want to be a good servant, so that means pushing on. If a mother wants a child, there is the pain of childbirth, dirty diapers, and sleepless nights as well as the joys that accompany being a mother. If a farmer wants a harvest, he will need to work the field and buy seeds. If I want to do the will of God and pull entire communities out of poverty, I need to expect and accept trials and hard times. A good mother doesn't abandon her children, and a good farmer doesn't call it quits in July. Further, good mothers and farmers learn from the past and fulfill their duties with wisdom and constancy. Likewise, if I am going to be an Economic Missionary, I need to also learn from the past and operate more wisely in the future. It would be insanity for me to assume that everything was going to proceed as planned. I am not being realistic if I don't recognize that my trials as an Economic Missionary will be significantly greater than those that I had as the president of an advertising agency. By clearing these bigger obstacles, I become much stronger and can operate well into the future. For me, the emotional payday of doing God's will and something this cool far outweighs any troubles that I may encounter. Not only do I need to accept the troubles I encounter, but I need to embrace them as part of the journey.

Smaller Factories – A potential solution

I am not entirely giving up on Haiti, although I will need to operate differently. Instead of having the big factory on the hill, we may consider operations in a series of smaller buildings. We learned not to be ostentatious in Haiti but we may also consider implementing this in other countries. If we are less ostentatious, maybe we can become less of a target. Maybe smaller factories will allow us to fly under the radar. Further, if one gets destroyed, we may have other ways to keep people employed.

I love the wonderful and determined people who made the Praville Economic Mission concept a reality. I want to go back and help these people. The reality is that I can't return until a legitimate government is in place and they are strong enough to have a police force that is effective. Further, thousands of formerly decent young adults are now murderers, crooks, kidnappers and rapists. Even after a government is in place, these gang members will still be criminals and they will still have their automatic weapons. I can't see how I can responsibly return in the near future and it may take 20 years or more before Haiti returns to something that resembles a civilization.

Never Waste a Good Failure

Looking back, it was probably risky to have four hundred solar panels and a $400,000 solar energy system on a hill surrounded by starving and impoverished people. Although most of the locals understood what we were doing, it was risky. In our defense, I made the decision to put the mission in Praville before Haiti slid into a virtual lawless nightmare. During the construction period, and the first 6 months of operation, Haiti was considerably more secure than the final months of operation. As I move forward, I continue to understand that risk is real and risk will always be involved. The reality is, if we are very successful, our mission may have a multitude of factories and quite possibly, we may realize something similar to the terrorist attack in the future. It would be foolish to see it as something that could never happen again.

Unfortunately, I can't let my employees off so easily. As their neighbors dismantled our factory, they did nothing. They maintained friendships with the same people that destroyed their livelihood and they never expressed how they felt. Our security was nowhere to be found. Even after the AK-47s left the site, the people who were benefiting most from the factory did nothing. To me, that was one of the most disheartening aspects of the terrorist attack. I can forgive them, but I can't forget that they would not be there to protect the factory in any capacity if this were to happen in the future. I still stand behind my statement that my wonderful employees worked miracles and they are still a group of people that I love very much. That notwithstanding, the massive display of cowardice still bothers me today.

I understand the pillaging of my factory by my neighbors. Anger over an unfair government, starvation, and gang violence for years at a time has horrible side effects. Given a choice between feeding their family with food provided by the gang and taking a noble path to starvation, my neighbors did what they perceived they had to do. That is the side effect of violent desperation. They knew they were destroying their future but they had to eat today and they thought that selling my machines would help them. I have a hard time judging my factory neighbors because I have never been that hungry nor have I ever been that frightened. In that scenario, I think I would have made the same choice. It is unwise to say what we would have done in that situation when that situation is unimaginable.

SIDE STORY

One way to make flying better

I have talked with missionaries that loved being in Haiti. I don't get it. Although I enjoyed many of the people I met, Haiti is perhaps my least favorite place on earth. After being trapped behind convent walls for days on end, nothing felt better than a window seat on a jetBlue airplane heading back home. There was no dust, violence or street noise. My seat was comfortable, and there was air-conditioning. With a little luck, I was able to talk the flight attendant into getting me a snack and a glass of wine before takeoff. The airport was dirty and hot but at least I felt safe there, but the airplane on the way home was amazing.

The Vision of the Ultimate Upside

What is driving me forward is the fact that we have a viable way to employ thousands of people and maybe even more. What excites me and my partners is that the payroll that was paid to one employee was working to move as many as 50 people across the UN's extreme poverty line. I don't sleep at night and it isn't because of fear. My heart races because if God opens up the doors that allows us to employ 5000 people, I wonder if that really means that we can pull 200,000+ people out of extreme poverty. On a small scale, that is what happened when a steady flow of payroll was injected into the local community. It would take committed people who are smarter than me. It would also take a small army of Angel Investors, but I am convinced that God can guide me to the brainpower and financing required to do his will.

We weren't flawless and we had lots of headaches. We naïvely went into this entirely inexperienced and in the first year of operations, we exceeded the wildest expectations. Truth is, we turned away business because we couldn't manage it. A friend of mine opened up a pizza place with minimal experience and it took him 3 years to formulate a great pizza that people loved. I humbly submit that mass-producing a polo shirt is harder than making an exceptional pizza. God was with us and we were well ahead of the curve. If by the will of God, the Economic Mission concept would expand, whether I am integrally involved or not, the degree of joy that I would experience would be beyond comparison. I would give my all to that effort, in any way I could, until the day I die.

Accepting and even embracing the bad things that happened to me and understanding that more bad things will happen in the future are survival mechanisms. I also understand that these "bad things" can train us to be better in the future. I recognize now, more than ever, that by accepting the bad with the good things that happen, I can grow and even succeed to higher levels. We can't control the world around us but we can control our response. We also need to accept the possibilities of what God can do with our mission and be open to something that is bigger than we could ever imagine. Amor Fati – we will accept whatever comes our way!!!

6 - ENDING HOPELESS POVERTY

*One Economic Mission can end hopeless
poverty for thousands of people.*

Ending poverty for thousands of people is an enormous goal but nonetheless possible. The Economic Mission is the most effective way to help impoverished people due to its permanence and its ability to combat the root causes of poverty. In areas with an Economic Mission, we fully expect that extreme poverty will end for a vast majority of people in the local economy. As paydays come and go, we expect prosperity to build on a weekly basis and more of the population to be lifted out of extreme poverty. There is a cumulative effect of payroll being spent repeatedly when that money hits the street. Each time a dollar is spent, it is helping somebody. While Economic Mission cannot eradicate all of the world's extreme poverty, it can create significant change for the lives for many people who are in close proximity to our factory. It is important to note that people who do not participate in local commerce or get jobs as they are created will not benefit from the Economic Mission.

About Safe Decisions

The political environment for 501(c)(3) organizations requires them to always do what is right and to be virtually flawless. These organizations are often graded in hindsight and in a social media world that isn't friendly. One of the first lessons I learned in business to business marketing is that managers will make the safe choice long before they make the best choice. The result is that in spite of the Economic Mission model being far superior, it is difficult for 501(c)(3) leaders to do what's best because they are required to do what is safe.

This photo sums up everything. Emencie and her coworkers dedicated themselves to becoming skilled sewing machine operators that could produce very high quality and low cost polo shirts. We are thankful to Boyer's Markets in Orwigsburg, Pennsylvania who took a chance on us and became our first corporate customer. Melissa at Boyer's is looking great in her uniform shirt!

Investors Fare Better

People who invested in our Economic Mission have delighted in the fact that they were providing opportunity instead of feeding one person one time. Reports of the Ripple Effect of payroll delighted our Angel Investors. Investors loved empowering people and the long-term prospects that training and employment provide. Concepts like replacing dependency with dignity went a long way. These people made significant investments while looking for significant long-term change in a deeply impoverished community. In Praville, we proved we were able to do that, and our investors, like our employees, founders, and support network, all loved being part of it. We found something, and it is scalable.

It is safe and logical to say the Economic Mission model provides a more effective use of funds for an investor than it would for an NGO donor in 5 profound ways.

1. In a traditional NGO, donations to feeding programs are literally gobbled up and gone. The next day, new donations are required so these benefactors can be fed again and again. By providing opportunity via an Economic Mission, employees successfully feed themselves on a daily basis. Further, in the process of feeding themselves they drive an economic engine that ripples throughout the community so their neighbors can also feed themselves.

2. An NGO or 501(c)(3) provides very little ripple effect. Except for a small portion of funds that is paid to local workers, revenue is gobbled up by benefactors and that is all a donation can do. An Economic Mission provides waves of paydays. Each payday steadily moves more of the surrounding community out of extreme and hopeless poverty. In a small community with an

Economic Mission, employees who spend money are an enormous benefit to their neighbors.

3. By investing in an Economic Mission, paying for the traditional middleman services of and NGO or 501(c)(3) are eliminated. Virtually every cent of every investment is poured into the manufacturing capabilities and capital requirements needs of the Economic Mission.

4. Many NGOs have schools. Unfortunately, without opportunity, the benefit of an education is greatly diminished. Haiti is replete with NGO supported schools that provide educations of varying quality. Too frequently, the result is the same, where students graduate without a chance of ever finding a job. In the Economic Mission model, there is a focused and robust adult training program. Every employee that completes the training gets a job. We are not suggesting that a traditional education is wasted, but instead, the Economic Mission clearly provides better opportunity.

5. Finally, as the Economic Mission is profitable, the Angel Investor's original investment can be returned to the investor, or it can be rolled over to provide opportunity in another place ravaged by extreme poverty and violent desperation. In the NGO model, every dollar is used once and is gone forever.

It is easy to see how an investment in an Economic Mission, when possible, is the most effective way an investor can eliminate abject poverty. Providing opportunity will always outperform providing relief!

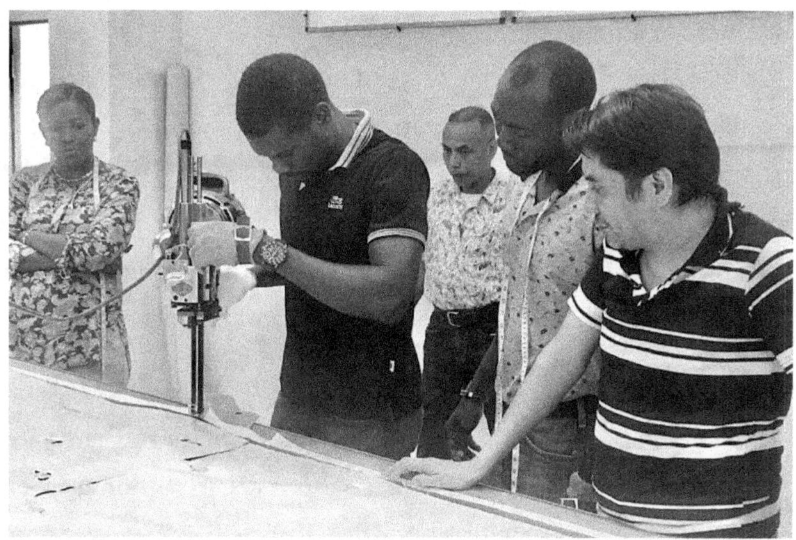

This is Blonncy Charles making the first ceremonial cut in the fabric so we could begin production at the factory in Praville. Blonncy was a very spiritual man and was one of my favorite employees because he possessed a quiet and humble drive to be great. He also made me laugh.

Employees Fare Better

The Economic Mission is better for employees. I have seen food distribution, and I know what it looks like. The poorest of the poor check their dignity at the gate and go into a facility where they are processed and given their ration. Unfortunately, as they pass the gate on the way back out, they are unable to pick up their dignity. It's gone. Here are 3 ways employees fare better in an Economic Mission environment.

1. People are not created to be useless. Employees of the Economic Mission have dignity and even self-esteem. Employees are

winners who can take care of themselves. They don't need to grovel or beg. Further, they have a personal pride in their ability to provide for themselves. Finally, because we informed them, they have self-esteem because they know that spending their paychecks helps the community around them. They also understand that by being successful, they are paving the way for others to be hired. No NGO delivers this kind of dignity.

2. Previously in this book, we discussed relative poverty. Our employees enjoy relative wealth. Trainees who never had $30 in their pockets become employees who receive $80 on a weekly basis. While their neighbors are living $10-$15 a week, our employees are averaging $60 – $90 per week. Our employees live in "relative prosperity". No NGO can provide prosperity while staying in budget. Our employees were able to see a dentist or a doctor when they needed. They could weather-proof their house and enjoy better meals. Further, our relatively wealthy employees were routinely generous and shared their "fortunes" with the extremely poor.

3. Many Christians will suggest that keeping Christ in the center of their lives during the busy workday is often difficult. In this regard, our employees fare better than most of their US counterparts. There are daily devotions and Christian music was often played during work. Our employees understand and embrace the fact that they are doing the work of God by making polo shirts. Christ was at the center of our mission and that benefited our

employees enormously. For my partners and me, this might be the most rewarding part of our Economic Mission.

As an Economic Mission Angel Investor, I get a thrill visualizing paydays. I love knowing that on payday, we pay our debt to our wonderful employees. I see the dignity that our Economic Mission provides. I love envisioning relatively wealthy employees leaving our factory and using a portion of their hard earned pay to help their poor and desperate neighbors. I love knowing that employees can have birthday parties and put shoes on the feet of their children. I love knowing that their payroll is spent over and over again in quick succession with each dollar helping people who desperately need it. Finally, it is especially rewarding to know that our Economic Mission is "making disciples in ALL nations"… At least all of the nations that our Economic Mission is touching. For people who want to feel good about doing something amazing, investing in an Economic Mission is clearly an excellent choice.

The Community Fares Better

The Economic Mission is better for the community. Where our Economic Mission was, providing daily relief would have been impossible. Because of the impossibility of relief, NGOs and 501(c)(3) organizations had lists of people they would help and others were excluded. Economics is the study of scarcity. The economics forced organizations to choose who got fed and who went hungry.

Sadly, every relief program, including Economic Missions, has people that are left out. There was a convent next to my factory that provided food for hundreds of people on a weekly basis. They also fed 750 students every school day. The nuns worked tirelessly to feed thousands of people every week. Unfortunately, the multitude of kids that were not in school and the people that were not in the feeding program, were left out and went hungry. Likewise, our Economic Mission will get one thousand applications for forty jobs. (We don't even advertise that we are hiring.) That is 800 people that didn't get interviewed and 960 people that do not get hired and are left out.

The good news is that every Friday, when $8,000 hits the streets, many of the people that didn't get hired will still benefit indirectly through the ripple effect when employees spend money. The Economic Mission helped push people across the UN's extreme poverty line and some entrepreneurs even did better than that. I take solace in knowing that even the people who didn't get jobs had a chance to live better because the factory was in town. If the factory had an additional year to mature, I believe that the area around our factory would have been fertile ground for micro-finance and we will hold that as a goal for the future.

Hot Dog Giveaway

As the factory construction was coming together, I would purchase 1,000 hot dogs and little packs of cookies and give them away. I wanted people who weren't yet getting jobs to have an appreciation for what a factory could do in their community. During the hot dog giveaway, hungry people came from everywhere and it probably took less than 15 minutes to give it all away. As my employees got their first bonus, I asked them to contribute to the next hot dog giveaway. I assumed they had a meeting because 100% of the employees gave back half of their bonus so we could buy hot dogs as a goodwill's gesture towards the community. It was awesome to see our company culture in action. It was extremely rewarding for me to see that some of the employees that were handing out hot dogs used to be people that were clamoring for hot dogs during previous hot dog giveaways. Employees were sharing their wealth and living their faith. For me and my partners, that was a victory to the highest degree.

It Isn't All Upside

Nobel prize-winning economist Milton Friedman would talk about how difficult choices can't exist without having negative consequences on both sides of the decision. In other words, if there is no downside, there isn't really a decision. There are several challenges that are unique to an Economic Mission. I may have been overly enthusiastic in extolling the remarkable benefits of the Economic

Mission. Genuinely eliminating hopeless poverty is beyond rewarding, and I highly regard it over simply stroking a check.

Here are some of the challenges facing our Economic Mission:

→ One big issue that we faced was opening a US-based sales unit to pull people out of poverty in Haiti. Somehow it is far more difficult than hiring a sales manager and letting the salespeople do their magic. I didn't keep my eye on the US sales effort, and I paid dearly for that. It is warehousing, inventorying, marketing, and shipping among a bunch of other challenges. Candidly, we initially made a lot of mistakes, and that was very expensive. We learned and we are getting it right. We find solace in realizing that we won't be soliciting donors for dead-end dollars year after year. Instead, we will be providing value to companies who benefit from our products.

→ Another issue pertains to management. The Economic Mission needs someone to ensure the factory is maintaining standards. It would be irresponsible for the president of the Economic Mission to collect funds from investors and take a casual approach to management of the factory. This means traveling with frequency to the factory. With all of Haiti's crime, traveling was extremely dangerous but necessary. There are no shortcuts. It takes commitment to make six or eight trips per year to a foreign country. It is important to have a daily phone call with the general manager and a conference call with the management team at least once a week.

→ My investors were great and supportive. Every once in a while, I would either call or write a status email, and they appreciated that. I believed it was crucial to be honest and discuss both the positives and negatives. Investing in an economic mission can be both exciting and rewarding for investors.

SIDE STORY

Angry Eighth Graders

I have a confession to make. Personally, I feel more comfortable interacting with older children and teenagers rather than young children or infants. On my first trip to Haiti, we visited a school towards the end of the school year. Everybody, except for me, was attracted to the cute and smiling 1st grade students while I went to see the 8th grade students. The little kids were happy and playful, but the 8th grade students were clearly dour and even fearful. When asked about their attitude, the 8th grade students responded that in a couple days school would end and they would no longer be eligible to participate in the school feeding program. In essence, they were moving from a group of people being fed to the group that was being left out. They rightfully feared hunger that could last for the rest of their lives because the NGO didn't have resources to feed them. Their educations were essentially useless because there was no opportunity. That reality was alarming because it forced me to recognize that the millions of meals we were providing via a school feeding program wasn't making the long-term difference for which we were hoping.

Paradoxes

There are a few paradoxes that help define the essence of the mission:

→ We invested in automatic/robotic machinery where the core benefit was that the owner could reduce labor. Remember, we are a company where payroll isn't an expense but an output. We made a significant investment in technology because we believed it drove our price/quality proposition. Our feeling was that if 530 million polo shirts were being purchased, having better quality and prices would help us get a larger market share and facilitate the necessity of hiring more people. The scarcity wasn't in the number of shirts we could make.

→ We had to make tough decisions for the sake of the mission. We found that Economic Mission employees will bring horrible stories, expecting them to be solved with the company checkbook. As an American who just built a factory, I was seen as a person with an unlimited supply of money, and our employees want it. One employee asked me flat out for $25,000 to change their life. This behavior is the employee looking to turn the Economic Mission into an NGO and for life to become easy. I like to think every human would prefer to work for what they get instead of receiving a handout. I probably need to adjust my expectations. Excuses are formulated with expertise on why an employee should miss work and still get paid. It wouldn't be accurate to claim that I never did anything for our employees. But every time I did something generous, I felt I was on a slippery slope that could lead to mediocrity and could produce NGO standards.

A Consumer Approach to Humanitarian Efforts

Ending poverty is a better value for the savvy and frugal investor. As consumers, we demand value and love bargains. To get a bargain, savvy consumers research, shop around and negotiate. But in a quirky turn of events, these same savvy consumers stop demanding value when it comes to charitable giving. Numerous NGOs and© 501(c)(3) organizations have successfully shifted the focus on themselves rather than prioritizing the beneficiaries they aim to serve. When it comes to the poorest of the poor, the focus must not shift away from the poor and hungry. As NGO donors become Angel Investors, the focus remains squarely on the community, the employees, and the payroll that ends poverty.

"Providing opportunity will always outperform providing relief."
Jim Weber

"In the middle of
difficulty lies opportunity.
Albert Einstein

7 - ECONOMIC MISSION OPERATIONS

The school of hard knocks has very expensive tuition.

As the president of a successful and slightly irreverent advertising agency, I was very good at writing proposals, entertaining clients, and keeping clients happy. I worked hard in the ad business, and there was pressure. Occasionally, we needed to land business so we could do raises or improve the life of myself and my fellow advertising agency employees. There was also the stress of ad agency deadlines, which I believe is part of the advertising business. I would always tell new hires that if they couldn't manage tight deadlines they should get out of the advertising business. That was as bad as it got being the president of an advertising agency. Looking back, it was pretty cushy because I had a wonderful group of accounts and entertaining them via golf outings, hockey games and martinis was probably more fun for me than it was for them. I also had a staff that I genuinely loved. It surely made me forget the stressful times where I had to hustle.

Unfortunately, my career as an Economic Missionary was difficult, thankless, dangerous, and became very stressful. Further, we began operations 3 months before the Covid outbreak. Further, I was opening an international business at the same time the world saw its worst shipping. I lacked experience in international business and textile manufacturing. I sought knowledge, best practices, and expertise. There were plenty of people who were helpful and I was learning, but nothing could fully prepare me for becoming a textile manufacturer in a Third World country. The school of hard knocks had very difficult classes and the tuition costs through errors got extremely expensive.

Further, Jennifer and I pumped the majority of our savings into the factory as we became the largest Angel Investor. Failure meant losing over half of the wealth we spent the last twenty-five years building. What kept me up at night was surprising. What weighed on me most was knowing I had the key to ending hopeless poverty and I needed to make the most of that. It got personal. I respected people like Exode and Eloi. These 2 employees were some of the most virtuous people I have ever met in my life. I loved the people on the production line and everybody who was doing their best to make the factory successful. If I failed, Praville would immediately slide back into hopeless poverty and there would be no opportunity to advance the Economic Mission business model. With the chaos of manufacturing in Haiti, the criminal government, the emotional demand to succeed, and the financial stress, I had very few "comfortable" days.

THE OPERATIONS MODEL

The Economic Mission operations model is simple. There are incredible challenges in executing each step of the model, but the business model itself is very basic and understandable. It is this simplicity in the business model that made the project's success possible.

The basic model contained 6 basic components:

1. Building shipping containers of raw materials, which we call kits, are shipped to Haiti.

2. Upon arrival, the kit clears Customs and is moved to our factory ninety miles away.

3. Once everything is inventoried, polo shirts are made. When we get enough polo shirts to ship back to the US, they are shipped either via container or pallet using LTL (less than a full truckload) service.

4. When the shirts arrive in Miami, they become the property of the US sales unit. Upon arrival, the Haitian entity is credited for the value of the shirts. They are delivered to our warehouse and put into inventory in Lancaster, Pennsylvania.

5. As our US sales organization profitably sells the shirts,

they are embroidered, shipped, and billed through our US accounting office.

6. The proceeds from sales buy more supplies, pay payroll and operating expenses. The US office provides for capital purchases in the factory and eventually Angel Investor payback. As supplies are purchased, they are shipped to Miami, and the whole process starts over again.

Here is a little more detail on some of the operations' components of our business.

Kit Shipping

Kits are twenty-foot or forty-foot shipping containers that have everything that was needed to begin and complete production of enough product to fill a shipping container. A forty-foot shipping container holds enough fabric and supplies to make about 45,000 shirts. Since we were making polo shirts, Tonya, my sourcing guru, would put the fabric, thread, buttons, hang tags, collar tags, neck tape, sewing needles, sewing machine oil, and everything else in the container. We often needed other little things, like miscellaneous tools, light bulbs, and ladders. We constantly strived to get the little things that were often forgotten. For example, we needed to remember enzyme packets for our septic tank, and we were always checking for supplies like toner or ink for our printers. Further, we were trying to predict which high mortality machine parts that we didn't have in stock might be wearing out. For example, we had a belt break; it actually closed our factory for several days until we got the part in at a cost of $1,000. The belt break hurt because we were spending more on rush shipping than we were paying for the part, and we stopped driving payroll, which is the core function of our Economic Mission.

Getting everything on the container without forgetting anything was stressful. Tonya was an incredible asset because she is detailed, patient, and good with last-minute requests. Perhaps one of our biggest challenges was in regard to ordering fabric. If it was being imported, we needed to be very proactive because fabric from South Korea might take six months from order date to arrival in Haiti. We needed to predict usage by colors and fabric style. If it was being made in the US, we would still need two months of lead time. The challenge was to make sure we had predicted everything correctly and to make sure that everything that was necessary was in the container. In Haiti, there is nowhere to go for a presser foot for an automated Juki placket maker. If one was needed, we had to get it there fast. Sometimes we would rush ship small parts to Fort Lauderdale and Rodney would inveigle people at the airport to take parts with them on their flight to Port-au-Prince. As a rule, if it wasn't in the kit, we were going to struggle and spend a small fortune to get it to the factory. The preparation, details and the fear of forgetting something made us all anxious each time we filled container.

In this photo, our Haitian employees are toasting our sourcing director Tonya Ortiz who was able to speed up the shipment and get our employees back to work a little more quickly. Shipping from all over the world to a remote part of Haiti was an unending nightmare.

SIDE STORY

Getting Back To Work

The shipping crisis caused a fabric crisis in our factory. We had a container arrive late and employees were out of work for almost two weeks as we waited for the fabric to arrive at the port, clear customs then ship to our factory. This was bad because employees lost their sense of security and some employees thought that we were going out of business. There is no unemployment, so this layoff hurt. When the fabric arrived, happy employees returned to work. At the end of their first day back, the employees had a party and celebrated the arrival of the fabric and the reopening of the production lines.

Production and Shipping

Here is where it is important to first act like a business. Target costs for production must be hit, mistakes must be eliminated, and hitting the spec must be mandatory. We had to be demanding and I was probably too nice. It is very hard to discipline someone that has lived such a hard life, and I didn't always do what I should have done. Employees rarely made mistakes from the heart, but those mistakes were hurting our ability to be competitive. We had to build a culture where employees believe everything must be perfect. Controlling costs and reducing mistakes were necessary for us so we could remain price competitive. We were also under pressure to maintain quality because we believed that was how we were going to keep the large customers that we had. It is almost like we got our large clients too quickly and we needed to get very good very quickly so we could keep benefiting from those large and profitable relationships. To maintain a level of several hundred employees, significant output and sales that only come through reorders from major clients are needed. For us, a major client would be someone who ordered 30,000 shirts or more per year.

We had room for improvement in each category, and we had our failures. With only one or two production lines, paying for trainers and management took up more of our budget than we would have liked, so we often missed our target cost for labor. We made huge production mistakes. We produced 15,000 shirts that were all "out of spec", or with defective embroidery, which cost us $100,000 and frustrated our second largest client. Getting Third World people to think like managers and control a situation will be an uphill battle. Haitian schools and culture are completely void of creative thinking. As 15,000 grossly undersized shirts were coming off the line, nobody stopped to measure the spec. When asked why, people on the production line basically said that they were given the shirts to sew and they did the job to the best of their ability. The positive thing was that Haitians generally do what they are told without arguing or complaining. No matter where we operate, each culture will have unique nuances, and we need to manage that.

US Sales

Remember one very essential thing: THE WHOLE BUSINESS MODEL DEPENDS ENTIRELY ON THE ABILITY OF THE US SALES OFFICE TO SELL EVERYTHING THAT THE FACTORY MAKES. In our first year of sales, we targeted both small and large clients, and every order was sacred. I wasn't selling nearly as much as I needed to. Small contracts were killing me. I was paying $25,000 a month to sell products that the factory could produce in 3 hours. The result was that inventory was building too quickly and our cash was getting tied up in inventory.

I created a new sales and marketing plan. We put selling small quantities (fewer than 250 shirts) at the top of the Stop Doing List. We recently uncovered the disturbing fact that our US embroidery room could not embroider as many shirts as our factory could make, so we were destined to fall behind. We found new ways and new partners who want our product. We invested in a more aggressive marketing effort targeted only to wholesale and large uniform customers. We exhibited at trade shows, and we refocused so large customers are our main concern. Having large accounts has its drawbacks too. Our margins tumbled, but our costs per shirt tumbled also. If we lose a large customer, it will have a negative effect on the payroll that we can put on the street in Praville. However, with large customers, we will be selling most of what we are making and not paying for product to sit in a warehouse.

Proceeds & Profits from US Sales

It is important to have an understanding with investors that reinvestment back into the Economic Mission is essential for success; therefore the loan payback is a lengthy process. In times of inflation, investment may be a difficult request because their investment will be worth less over time. We used proceeds from sales to vastly expand our fabric inventory in Haiti. We feel that during this shipping crisis, we would have a distinct advantage over our Chinese competitors if we could add timely delivery to our price and quality value proposition. We also used our proceeds to purchase an automated placket machine and software that drastically reduced our fabric costs. This provides an example of the central goal of making sure the Economic Mission stays ultimately competitive so it can continue to increase production and market share.

Our Elevator Pitch

An elevator pitch is a concise description of what our company does in about the same time it takes to ride an elevator. Our elevator pitch is about seventeen seconds: We are an Economic Mission that produces high-quality and low-cost polo shirts that are shipped to the US to be sold as uniforms or for retail sale. Our mission pulls employees and communities out of hopeless poverty. Our quality is comparable to any brand sold in Macy's, and we routinely beat the prices from China.

There are several components to our elevator pitch that merit additional discussion:

High Quality – Building a culture that produces high-quality products in a Third World country is difficult. The term "quality" is relative in that it means different things to different people. For people living in Praville, quality in a polo shirt means only a few small holes. We needed to close the gap between what Americans and the Third World perceive quality to be. We needed to quantify what quality was for each operation. Each operator knew what quality meant for their job. This made training extremely important.

Low Cost – We found that if we expected companies to purchase our products on a continual basis, we needed to be at a price that they perceived as very competitive. We could get a "donation sale" in small volumes at high prices, but our employment goal at our Economic Mission is driven by volume. By "donation sale," I mean that a person or company would be willing to pay more than they usually do for a small quantity or a onetime purchase. Volume is driven by price and quality. We developed a "Vacated Expense Business Model" that allowed us to basically sell shirts slightly higher than the cost of materials plus the cost of labor. Our vacated business model will be discussed in more detail later in the book.

Shipped to the US – It is important for us to view our Economic Mission as an exporting entity and to remember that everything that the factory makes must be sold. This will be discussed in detail later in the book. There were companies and schools in Port-au-Prince that would have purchased our second-quality shirts to be used as uniforms since Haiti law requires all school students to have a uniform. We could have easily won much of that business, but in doing that, the people who made shirts for those customers would lose their livelihoods; we would only be transferring jobs to our factory and not truly adding jobs. Instead, we donated our second-quality shirts to organizations that help people after natural disasters, like the earthquake. On the aggregate, countries that export do better than countries that can't export. We feel that we can do the most good as an exporter.

Business Before Charity – The owners and top management of this company need to constantly remind themselves that they are not an NGO (non-governmental organization) or a 501(c)(3) nonprofit. A business operates entirely differently than an NGO. A business wants to gain market share and build profits, while an NGO defines excellence by helping people. A Third World NGO rarely demands excellence from the people they are helping. The company, on the other hand, must demand a high degree of excellence and accountability from every employee in order for the organization to remain competitive on a price and quality basis. Employees that don't want to be held accountable will remind managers and owners that the mission is to pull them out of poverty.

Narrow Scope of Products – We desire to be one of the best manufacturers in the world of solid-colored, wicking polyester, self-collared polo shirts. We believe we are on the path to achieving that goal. Further, the positive aspect of the attack on our factory permits us to take all of the lessons we learned and build a factory that is even more efficient and serves our unique needs perfectly. In our new factory, we need to continue to improve processes and skills. We selected a product that has significant demand in the US so we wouldn't need to add any other products to our offering. In the book, Good to Great, Jim Collins points out that in order to be successful in a business venture, businesses should strive to be the very best in the world at what they are doing. We desire to be the best in the world at making polo shirts and delivering them in a "Less Than Container Load" (LCL) so our big customers can order five thousand to ten thousand shirts at a time, saving warehouse space and capital costs.

Equipment Specialization – In Haiti, there are several companies that could make polo shirts. Every polo shirt has a placket, which is the front of the shirt with the buttons. Because these companies don't specialize in polo shirts, they don't have an automated placket-making machine like we do. It isn't worth the $50,000 investment for them. This gives us the opportunity to be more efficient and have the highest quality plackets possible. By specializing, we are able to have the right equipment that helps us be the best in making our narrowly focused products.

Maintenance Expertise – In Third World countries, maintenance of machinery and infrastructure is a significant challenge. Like any factory, we have an array of varied pieces of equipment requiring maintenance and repair know-how. In other words, in the Third World, the same guy that repairs the sewing machines also repairs the elevator, the air conditioner, the solar power plant, the compressor, and a host of other pieces of equipment. When something breaks, picking up the phone and getting expert service is not an option. By narrowing our product offerings to polo shirts, we have reduced the number of complex machines for our maintenance person to manage. Although our maintenance person has technical schooling, it is not to the same standard as developed countries. Our maintenance man relies on how to videos on YouTube, but he can only get it if the Internet is working on that day, and it can only help to a certain degree.

Staff Specialization – We trained our first production line at an external training center funded by USAID. We then brought them to our factory and trained them for an additional six weeks. During that time, we analyzed each employee and their skill effort. In making a polo shirt, there are high-, medium-, and low-skill operations. By specializing, we are able to keep operators improving on a small number of tasks so they continue to improve their quality over time. If we jumped to pants, dresses, or hats, we would require new operations, and our operators would be less skilled at those varied operations. There will be more on training later in the book.

Responsiveness – By producing only polo shirts, we are able to have more fabric in stock, which allows us to quickly respond to the demands of our US customers. It can take about twenty-four weeks from order date to get fabric to arrive in Haiti. Further, each container has a value of $90,000 or more. By not manufacturing other products, we are able to carry larger inventories of the fabric we use to make polo shirts. This drastically improves the chances that when the sales office calls with an order, we can produce it without having to order more fabric, and we can get it to our customer quickly.

Sales Expertise – By limiting our production to polo shirts, our sales office can develop a set of skills that helps them sell to large customers better. They know what clients to seek out and how to seek them out. They understand sizing and grading and are getting good at predicting reorders.

Self-Sufficiency/Vertical Integration

A friend and client of mine was a farm equipment dealer. He always said that "farmers need to control the factors they can." As it relates to our factory, worrying about hurricanes or government issues is a waste of time and energy because we can't control it. We should only focus on the things we can control. Vertical integration allows us to control more of the factors that we can. Vertical integration as part of the Economic Mission is more about controlling the factors instead of gaining additional margin. However, additional margin means that we can be even more competitive. The small steps that we took toward vertical integration paid off significantly. For example, it cost us $31,000 to implement our own marker system. (A marker tells the people that are cutting the fabric where to cut.) When we took over all aspects of that, we could turn product faster, deliver more accurate sizing, and reduce costs. We became more competitive.

Not everybody shares our passion for excellence and quality. When we relied on Haitian sources to help complete manufacturing tasks, disaster and reduced quality often followed. Controlling more factors means extra capital is required to buy the machinery. It also means extra training and extra headaches. We learned about the value of vertical integration the hard way, but our first factory was too small to add anything else. Our future factories will benefit from what we learned in Haiti and from a higher degree of vertical integration.

Here are some ways we can vertically integrate and gain better control of factors in the future:

→ In our new factory, we are buying yarns that are the colors of the shirts we are making. We are also buying the circular knitting machines and post-knitting machinery required to make our own fabrics. By procuring yarns of three different deniers (filaments and thicknesses), we will gain the ability to produce every fabric that we use. This will give us greater flexibility and shorter turnaround times. Further, we will be able to do custom fabrics and thicknesses per our customers' spec. Customers will love exact specifications with a quick turnaround.

→ We will generate our own electricity via a combination of solar energy and backup generators. It is hard to have confidence in third-world electric providers and their ability to power a factory with consistent levels of clean electricity. Moreover, electricity in 3rd world countries is created by using diesel generators making it very costly.

→ We will vigorously train our maintenance people, and each maintenance person will have specialties, so we don't need to go to outside services for repairs and maintenance. We are sending our people to the United States for this training.

→ We made the decision to operate as a Christian-oriented Economic Mission. We found that security companies don't treat people in a Christian manner. Further, they don't follow policy and these people are usually under paid. Their demeanor and attention to detail shows that. We employ a joyful yet professional security crew.

→ Although this isn't exactly vertical integration, we will hire one quality person to act as our truck driver. Changing truck drivers is a security risk, and deliveries aren't made as promptly as we desire. We will pay slightly better, and our driver will always take care of us first or we will find someone else that will.

→ Our boxes continue to crush and look bad on pallets, which isn't good for us in the eyes of our customers. We will establish our own box-making capabilities in our new factory so we can affordably manufacture boxes that are crush resistant.

→ Using an outside embroidery company cost us over $32,000 because they didn't get the quality right and we didn't want to sell the shirts. Further, they were clear that they didn't care because they already got paid! (That is 3rd world business.) In the future, we will manage our own embroidery processes, and the people we hire will care about quality.

Vertical integration significantly adds to startup costs but also enhances our factory's competitiveness and allows for better quality. We believe that by improving the responsiveness to our customers and by delivering higher quality products, we can increase opportunity employments and achieve a higher payroll. Remember, in an Economic Mission, payroll is an output, and delivering price and quality is what drives that payroll. Vertical integration enhances our competitive edge and contributes to our ongoing success.

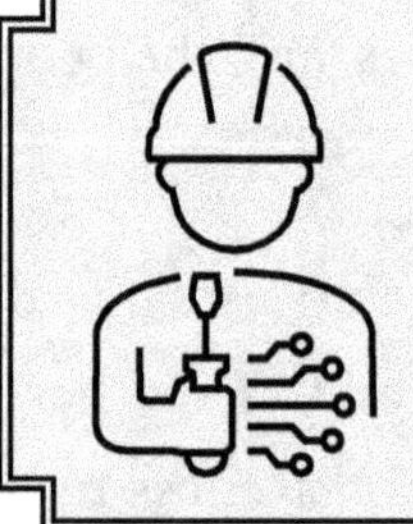

"Work gives you meaning and purpose and life is empty without it."
Steven Hawking

8 - SELLING WHAT THE ECONOMIC MISSION MAKES

EVERYTHING THAT IS MADE BY THE FACTORY *MUST BE SOLD.*

When I was sixteen years old, my dad had a poster on his office wall and forty-three years later, it hangs in my office. The message on the poster pointed out how critical sales are to the financial health of any business. It is interesting that my dad was a chemical engineer, but his company was highly successful by getting everybody to understand the necessity of sales. Like any business, robust sales remain a critical necessity for our Economic Mission. It is by creating demand for a product that the Economic Mission will be able to offer additional opportunities. Sales in the US will drive payroll at our factory. Without sizable sales and increasing demand, the Economic Mission is nothing more than a feel-good entity.

Sales in the United States made an enormous difference to our neighbors in Praville, Haiti. With one production line, it seems like we were doing good things for our employees, but we weren't able to significantly impact the lives of our neighbors. An aggregate payroll of $4000-$5000 wasn't enough to significantly improve

Praville as a whole. Although it improved some of our neighbors' lives, the improvement wasn't holistic. As sizable orders came in, we trained and employed 30+ additional employees so we could begin operations on a 2nd production line.

As we added the 2nd production line, we seemed to push close or past critical mass where we could begin to noticeably improve the community around the factory. Since most of the people in Praville are living in extreme poverty, it didn't take an enormous amount of payroll to start making a difference. The reality is that getting one person across the UN's $2.15 extreme poverty line isn't that difficult or even expensive. The process of helping thousands to cross the extreme poverty line takes a steady flow of payroll to act as an injection of cash for the vicinity around the factory. This process didn't need managed. As long as we were meeting payroll, employees were spending money and our nonemployee neighbors were doing better.

If payroll being spent over and over again was achieving a multiplier of 5, which many economists consider conservative, approximately 7,000 extremely poor people were sharing $40,000 in extra spending power each and every week. If that was happening, 7,000 people were averaging an extra $.81 a day. That may seem paltry, but when local Haitians were living on $1.50 per day, $.81 is a 54% increase in their daily purchasing power! For many, that extra $.81 was the difference between self-sufficiency and malnutrition. The ones who did better than average were able to buy clothing and repair their roofs. Since there was virtually no government, we had no way of knowing how many were financially impacted by our factory nor did we know the exact extent, but it was obvious that life was getting better because there was a steady flow of payroll. All of that happened because we were able to sell our product.

For the multitude of street vendors, their lives improved to a greater degree. As we would add production lines in the future, that number would grow and food insecurity for locals would further diminish. Adding a 3rd production line would have continued to provide excellent results. I am convinced that payroll of $12,000 per week could have provided a "daily dollar" on average to every person in Praville. In one of the poorest parts of the world, an extra dollar every day in a sustainable fashion would change lives. It was the ripple effect of steady payroll that was making the difference. Sales in the US would be the exclusive driver that would demand that we add a 3rd production line.

Underselling was a threat to that flow of cash. About half of our cash was being used for payroll, so we needed to drive $16,000 per week in revenue to the factory in order to make $8000 in payroll. Our US sales operation needed to sell our shirts at a profit so they could pay for their expenses. To be hypercompetitive, we never wanted to drive large profits through our factory or US sales office. Our goal was to win business on a quality/price proposition. As the founder, I was able to land large deals with major companies but our US small contract operation severely underperformed. In the broadest of strokes, the failure of US operations to pay for themselves was draining our supply of cash. Operating unprofitably could have made us an NGO instead of an Economic Mission.

In the Economic Mission business model, it is unique that the role of sales is to drive demand instead of maximizing profit. Pricing strategy changes because it becomes more about getting the sale without losing money so an increase in demand can be achieved. Profit takes a backseat. The salesperson becomes an Economic Missionary whose job it is to create demand so we can hire more people. We emphasized the mission philosophy and combating poverty in our sales process, so customers feel good on the inside when they buy our products.

Our Sales Strategy

The basic strategy for our sales was where I, as the founder, would sell major contracts of 25,000-100,000 shirts and also have a US sales office selling smaller quantities from an inventory that was warehoused in the US. We were willing to breakeven on major contracts, but we were hoping to be profitable on the smaller jobs that were being pulled from our local inventory. Even if we lost a small amount of money on a big contract, employing people in Haiti was what we wanted to do as an Economic Mission. We felt that this was God's will for our factory. We believed our smaller contract sales would have been profitable enough to subsidize any minor loss or breakeven scenario. This was how we were going to get our share of the 530 million polo shirts that were being sold in the US every year.

With two production lines, our factory could produce close to 250,000–275,000 polo shirts per year. To keep things in perspective, a five thousand polo shirt order would keep our 2 production lines busy for four to five days. Our large account sales produced a volume of just under 100,000 shirts. Our profit margins were small, but this is what allowed us to have a second line and allowed our Economic Mission to begin to bring the community surrounding the factory out of poverty.

LARGE CONTRACT SALES - Our contract sales effort was performing at levels that exceeded expectations. The future even looked better. Socially responsible companies loved what we were doing and we were able to land two significant contracts in our first year of operations. Because we were able to vacate so many expenses, we were able to match almost any price of any manufacturer in the world. We were able to help very large companies be socially responsible without it costing these companies more than what they were already paying. In some instances, we even produced a savings for these companies. We were very optimistic about this side of our business. We had two other large corporate players express an interest and we were actually delaying the sales process so our training and Haitian operations could mature to handle the influx of business. Contract orders from sizable companies were mind blowing. We learned that there were multiple companies that wanted shirts in quantities that would fill an entire shipping container. These orders could routinely exceed $250,000. For a young company with no experience to have this opportunity was clearly a godsend. Our factory handled these jobs well, but the difficulty of sourcing the fabric and other items required to fill these orders remain difficult due to lingering effects of Covid. Further, the international shipping crisis seemed to have no end in sight and was demoralizing to our staff. Our employees in Haiti were up to the challenge. Huge orders meant security for them. They never forgot that their jobs were an opportunity.

Pravi was able to sell two major accounts that consumed about seventy percent of the production from our first production line. Because of our mission and because of our commitment to being a low cost, quality provider, we were able to build a great relationship with a Fortune 500 company. Shortly after that, we made a deal with a worldwide fast food chain with thousands of locations. Both companies have the capability of annually placing multiple shipping container orders of 50,000 shirts or more. In retrospect, I am surprised that a brand-new company being run by someone with no textile experience was able to land two major clients this quickly. Our Economic Mission was attractive because of our mission and reduced environmental impact. During these pitches, I felt that God's hands were all over this mission.

<u>US SMALL CONTRACT SALES</u> - In contrast, our US small contract sales effort kept me humble. Our initial vision for the US sales operation was to sell our product in modest quantities of 50-1000 shirts. These shirts would be sold as uniforms to companies who wanted to save money on uniform costs while still getting a quality product. In essence, we were hoping to build a significant stock of shirts that would be turned 2 or 3 times annually. In between large orders, we would restock the warehouse and that would have a leveling effect on our production schedules. Simply put, when we were doing an order for 50,000 shirts, the US sales office would live off of the inventory. When the large contract was completed, we would restock the inventory, thus enabling us to keep everybody fully employed. If sales were strong, we could even afford to overproduce. This turned out to be more difficult than we thought it would be.

We struggled with implementing processes that were efficient. If we were going to sell everything the factory made, our local US sales effort needed to sell at least five hundred shirts per day. We were never in contention to hit that goal. Our GM struggled with implementing warehousing, service and embroidery processes. In spite of having a full time marketing employee, we struggled in the marketing realm. Our sales effort lacked creativity and we didn't come close to hitting the numbers that we needed to hit. The lofty salaries for 3 salespeople and a general manager quickly became a liability to the company. Eventually, and before the terrorist attack, the sales department was reduced to a single person. The single salesperson was excelling but not to the level that would allow us to sell everything we were making, therefore inventory was building to dangerous levels. When the factory was destroyed by terrorists, she resigned.

In summary, our smaller contract sales effort hurt our financial stability more than our large contract sales helped. As a result, we were churning cash. We learned that in the future, we need to either manage the small contract sales process better or learn to live without smaller contracts. The terrorist destruction of the factory provided us with the ability to hard stop what we were doing in smaller contract sales. Our largest accounts have invited us to pick up where we left off once we get a new factory. We can learn from our mistakes and operate differently. We can also set up our factory for higher volumes and vertical integration. In a sense, we are lucky, because of the terrorist attack on our factory, we now have an opportunity to stop and learn from our past failures.

The Power of Robust Sales

As a sales manager in the 1990s and a business owner in the 2000s, I always said, "There isn't anything great sales can't fix." That might be an overstatement, but when companies are driving great sales, everything else seems to fall in line. Higher and profitable sales can help companies keep employees. When sales are higher, disasters become more manageable. When sales are robust, buying equipment and staying out of debt is a reality. It is easy to remain highly competitive when there are robust sales. The entity can afford better marketing, technology, and people. Nothing helps an organization succeed like year-over-year sales growth.

As an Economic Missionary, I was thrilled to increase the number of people who were working in our factory. That came after we got large contracts. It is important to note that as an Economic Mission, maximizing profits isn't necessary. Since we are going for volume, we drastically reduced prices so we could get sizable contracts from great Fortune 500 companies and worldwide restaurant chains. Taking a lesser margin to get a deal done is part of the advantage of being an Economic Missionary. We still need to grow payroll more than we need profit, but we need to stay in a positive cash position. With aggressive pricing, transactions can go faster and customer acquisition is easier. Faster deals and ease of customer acquisition are addictive to salespeople. Salespeople like to win, and Economic Missionaries have advantages that other types of products or companies don't have.

We consider our prices, quality, and mission to be a significant part of a highly competitive value proposition that companies love. We recognize companies are people, and people generally want to do be gregarious. It is very important to note here that in many business to business transactions, employees are also looking for security. Middle managers almost always prefer the "safe" choices over "best" choices. The best choice may have risk, and employees that are afraid of making a mistake are genuinely risk adverse. In our sales process, this is the "secret objection."

The Takeaway from Our Mistakes

The takeaway is that no matter what product the Economic Mission is producing, a selling machine that can keep pace with your production must be created. If the sales effort can outpace production, the Economic Mission will need to grow, and thus be more impactful through expanded payroll. It would have been astonishing if somehow we could have gotten three hundred to five hundred employees in the challenging Haitian business environment. It would be amazing to see the impact that would come from $35,000 in payroll circulating in an environment where most people make less than $30 a month.

Golden Handcuffs

The Economic Mission has the key to "golden handcuffs", and this is important when recruiting salespeople! They are trapped by golden handcuffs when they make big income and are no longer free to do something meaningful because they can't afford a reduced income. At some point in almost every salesperson's life, they start wondering if life can be about more than the next sale. Good salespeople quickly climb Maslow's hierarchy of needs. After a couple bonus checks, they have gotten past Maslow's physical needs. They have taken care of the basics of fine dining, designer clothing, and a fancy place to live. Next on the hierarchy, they are safe and are building nest eggs for emergencies and retirement. Going to the next step in Maslow's hierarchy, outgoing salespeople usually can find love and friendship. As they become successful, they find esteem and even get the big house and fancy German car. Unfortunately, for the typical salesperson, Maslow's holy grail of self-fulfillment remains elusive. Over time, good salespeople find themselves asking if chasing the next sale is fulfilling. Many salespeople wonder if chasing the next commission check is the best version of who they can be. This is where golden handcuffs become confining. Many salespeople with fifteen years of sales experience would rather do something else, but they are committed financially to making the "big bucks," and they often find themselves trapped. The Economic Mission can offer good salespeople a unique opportunity where they can make very good money but live life with purpose.

The Inventory Dilemma

Rising inventory levels were counterproductive to our effectiveness. We have 75,000 shirts in a warehouse that cost us a little less than $6 apiece, after shipping and US sales costs. We generated $1.20-$1.50 of payroll in Haiti for every shirt, or a total of about $100,000. The problem is that we spent a fortune between production and sales to generate $100,000 of payroll in Haiti. Inventory buildup has an adverse effect on three levels. First, by tying up $450,000 in capital, we are greatly diminishing our ability to acquire assets that could make us more competitive. Second, with an excess of shirts, there is no need to hire or pay overtime because we have the inventory we need. Therefore, the payroll output objective is being minimized. Third, with lower profit margins, making up for past losses will take years. Of course our operation needs inventory so we can fill orders, but we can easily get by on a fraction of the inventory we have if we refresh our inventory on a biweekly basis. In essence, when the US sales office is screaming for product, the future looks bright for making life better for some very poor people.

What Is Branding?

A strong brand is simple. It is nothing more than attaching a product or company name to a meaningful benefit. For example,

Walmart is cheap, and Volvo is safe. Consumers expect to save money at Walmart and to be able to walk away from a car accident because they own a Volvo. Those are benefits. It is important to note that nothing disappoints consumers more than a company that breaks their brand promise. A consumer would be very disappointed if they saw a lower price on a product that they recently purchased at Walmart. Macy's doesn't have "lowest price" as a core part of their brand so customers would be more accepting of not paying the lowest price at Macy's. A brand that is unique or first to market is particularly strong, and it doesn't always need to take a lot to have a strong brand position. Enterprise Rent-A-Car became the nation's largest rental car company by simply promising to "pick you up".

The Pravi Brand

Pravi is the brand that pulls people out of poverty. We made sure that potential customers understood our tagline and that we were "The Polo Shirt With A Mission." We promoted a benefit where customers could look great outside and feel great inside. All people have goodness within them, and our brand taps into that goodness. Further, we wanted to be sure people understood the power they had when they purchased our products. A strong brand is who you are and not what you aspire to be. When we were at sales meetings, I told stories about people in Haiti and our factory and buyers connected with our mission.

Our Brand Advantage

By branding the polo shirts that we were making in Haiti, we were able to open up amazing opportunities. As I met with potential customers, I witnessed the power of our brand as we were able to land business that other companies would work years to get. Our customers were more accepting of things like a missed deadline because they knew that we were going through growing pains. It was crazy, but employees of the companies we were pitching actually became advisors and promoters of our company because they believed in our brand. Almost every sales call had somebody in the meeting who wanted to help our mission. Given time, we could have achieved considerably higher numbers than we were because our brand was so strong. Finally, our customers got more because instead of just buying uniforms, they felt like they were combating poverty and world hunger. Our customers got more because they felt great about their relationship with Pravi.

We believe our unique selling proposition was that a customer could get high-quality polo shirts without having to pay more for them, and their purchase would pull people out of poverty. Our unique selling proposition first gave the customer the quality shirt that they wanted. We then gave the customer a sense that they were part of something great.

Embedded in our brand is that we are Christian-based and doing the will of God. We found that being a Christian-based brand helped us more than it hurt us. We were simply saying who we are and what we stand for. We don't believe that an Economic Mission needs to be Christian-based, but we proudly are. We believe the mission gets us to the bargaining table. We still need to drive quality and price. We can't hide behind our mission or Christianity in lieu of delivering price and quality. Like Walmart or Volvo, we need to stick to our brand promise. The best part about our brand is that it is true and not contrived. We said what we did, and we did what we said. That is what strong brands do.

Using the Pravi Brand in the Sales Process

My first cold call sale was absolutely amazing and lots of fun. I went to PDQ Locks in Lancaster, PA. They are a sizable company that manufactures high-quality locks and other door accessories for exterior and interior doors. They sell a ton of them, and they could buy lots of polo shirts.

I recall being slightly nervous. I had invested my life savings into a factory, and now I was going to see if I could sell it. I walked through the front door and got to the gatekeeper. I smiled, looked her in the eye, and said, "I am Jim Weber, and I am an Economic Missionary." She asked me what that was, and I told her the whole story about me building a factory in Haiti and pulling people out of poverty by making polo shirts; now, as an Economic Mission-ary, I had to sell those polo shirts so I could continue to pull people out of poverty. I tried to keep it light and entertaining. I then told her that I needed to talk to whoever bought polo shirts for their company. Five minutes later, I was in the president's office talking with several executives who were interested in my mission, and I was informed that they bought a significant number of polo shirts. I proved my quality by having samples, and I told them I would hit any price that I needed to so I could pull my people out of poverty. I told them awesome stories about my people at the factory, and I made it clear that if they needed shirts, they were being impactful if those shirts came from the factory that pulls people out of poverty. They were good people and good businessmen. I don't believe they purchased extra shirts from me, but that they got what they needed at a great price and felt terrific about doing it.

SIDE STORY

The Joy Of Selling

It isn't for everybody, but sales can be fun and rewarding if you care about the company you are selling for and equally care for the customer you are selling to. As a trained salesperson, I understand how to close sales and even pressure customers. A long time ago, I abandoned that philosophy and instead I tried to become service oriented, which benefited my advertising agency enormously. Instead of selling what we had, I made our advertising agency what customers wanted. The result was that we were able to maintain 25-year customer relationships and my sales career was rewarding. I was never restrained by Golden handcuffs because I was enjoying life and I loved making a difference for my customer. I was different from other sales people and my customers appreciated that.

Every potential customer that I talked with loved what we did. I was very passionate about the Economic Mission, and therefore selling it became easy. In other words, I sold by using the brand benefit that we had. We wouldn't have an inventory problem if I would have hired an operations person and I hit the streets pushing product. In fact, in writing this book, I see this all too clearly. My benefit to this mission isn't my wisdom or insight. My core benefit is selling shirts and attracting Angel Investors, which is also selling. It was fun selling again, and I reached the pinnacle of Maslow's hierarchy of needs by doing something that was so meaningful. I realize I need to be a leader, but the big change for the future is that I will hire towards my weakness and I will do what I do best.

Sales & Marketing Plan

I think every company should have a Sales & Marketing Plan. This can be part of the business plan, but it needs to show a clear path for how the company is going to reach and sustain robust sales. Like any Sales & Marketing Plan, we isolated potential markets, assigned a level of sales for each market segment, and arrived at a potential market total. It defined how much capital would be needed and how many people it would take. In other words, the first part of my Sales & Marketing Plan was like any other plan. I would encourage anybody embarking on an Economic Mission to also write into the plan how they are going to become extremely successful.

In his book, Built to Last, Jim Collins discusses BHAGs (Big, Hairy, Audacious Goals). They are huge goals that drive progress and define a vision. It is about thinking big. For Grateful Inc., our BHAG is to employ thousands of people in multiple countries all in the same basic way. We want to build multiple factories in the center of impoverished, densely populated communities. We believe we would stay with textiles, but we may expand past polo shirts. We would also be interested in working with very large companies to provide production capacity for them. These companies need to share our goal that "payroll is an output instead of a cost," and we would need to hit their reasonable pricing targets.

We loved going to trade shows. Potential customers were very receptive to our selling proposition and we formed lasting relationships at trade shows. The people at the factory created an oversized shirt that was almost 5 feet wide and it garnered attention.

ESG Provides Opportunity for Economic Missions

Getting in the door at major corporations becomes easy for us because many of the world's largest companies are embracing ESG initiatives. ESG stands for Environmental, Social Responsibility, and Governance goals, which started out as a United Nations initiative but has since expanded. The environmental aspect addresses preserving the natural world, and things like lower gas emissions, carbon footprints and energy efficiency. Companies that are ESG sensitive love that we are one hundred percent operated with solar power. Our training program, in conjunction with our ability to pull people out of poverty, is very attractive to companies that are sensitive to human development and other social issues. The governance aspect deals with how we prevent corruption as well as investor compensation and management goals. We have two sentences that demonstrate how we are perfect ESG partners. "Our factory, Grateful Inc., is a 99.5% solar powered factory that pulls people out of poverty with a team of locally trained employees and managers who care deeply about producing high-quality polo shirts. The owner of the Economic Mission and their investors get no salaries nor do they draw any interest on the money that they have invested." Many companies have goals within their ESG initiative. For example, it is understood by me that Starbucks is favorable to female-owned companies. For companies that are sensitive to environmental issues and world poverty issues, we are an easy choice.

Many Fortune 500 companies have social compliance executives whose job it is to seek out partners that fit their ESG initiatives.

These companies are all very large and can provide sizable orders. Social compliance executives got us to the bargaining table so we had an opportunity to earn large contracts, but we had to earn the business through quality and price. Simply put, ESG executives will provide Economic Missions with the opportunity, but we had to earn the business. It is an enormous advantage to have our sales prospects rooting for us. Further, if our proposal is close to that of a non-ESG provider, we believe that we can usually get the contract or at least a chance to sharpen our pencil. Again, it is important for us to become a safe choice because buyers generally want job security on a personal level. As time goes by, if we become a safe choice with a 5 year history, we could expect large increases on a year-over-year basis. The challenge for us and any business in a similar fast-growing scenario will be to maintain quality. Our pricing challenges should soften as we benefit from large-scale operation.

We understand the urgency of selling everything we make. We need to do whatever we can to make that happen. The opportunity lies in our ability to be aggressive and increase demand through sales. We have a strong brand to get us in the door. We have great prices and quality, so we can be confident in repeat orders. In business to business applications, however, we need to be sure we are also a safe choice. Our mission will help some buyers emotionally "take a chance" on us.

"The man who will use his skill and constructive imagination to see how much he can give for a dollar, instead of how little he can give for a dollar, is bound to succeed."
Henry Ford

9 - SELECTING COUNTRIES AND FACTORY LOCATIONS

The location of an Economic Mission makes all the difference.

When asked why he robbed banks, famous bank robber Jesse James said that was where the money was. When I am asked why I went to Haiti, I similarly respond by saying Haiti is where the poorest people are. I went to Praville because that's where some of the poorest people in Haiti are. Over 30% of the population of Haiti is living below the UN's extreme poverty line. Praville was one of the poorest areas in Haiti, therefore we believed at least 70% of the Praville population was living on less than $2.15 per day. Praville is the poorest community I have ever visited. Haiti is where a little success would be most impactful. In Haiti, opportunity is rare and therefore by providing opportunity we can make a big difference. It is the hopeless poverty in Praville that made it possible for our Economic Mission to do so much good.

When selecting a location, it is wise to remain open and flexible and to minimize any preconceived notions or ideas. The missionary may be flying to a sunny country with a bunch of tourists, but when the plane lands, the tourists go one direction and he goes to a village that is in poverty. As locations for Economic Missions are selected, it is important to have criteria that help in the location selection process. In spite of the attack on our factory, location selection is the one thing that we got right. As Economic Missions open in the world's poorest locations, it needs to be understood that those locations have risks. People living in violent desperation will do what they need to do to survive and we need to live with this reality. Later in the book, we will discuss security. Location selection is about remaining objectively loyal to the mission and letting the Holy Spirit do the rest. It is about understanding the criteria. It is as much about saying no as it is about saying yes. A good location will make an impactful difference quickly and permanently.

Selecting a Country for the Economic Mission

When selecting the countries that could best utilize an Economic Mission, there are several considerations. If the goal is to remove people from hopeless poverty, areas where poverty is most hopeless provide the best opportunity. We have multiple sources of information that makes it clear which countries need our services most.

Per Capita GDP (PPP)

When accessing GDP (Gross Domestic Product) information online, we use information from the World Bank. It is important to stay consistent and use the same source for financial research whenever possible. GDP is the final value of all goods and services that are bought by the final user that was produced in a country. First, we look at per capita GDP, which tells us what the gross domestic product of a country is on a per person basis. When we saw Haiti's per capita GDP, we realized that they were clearly the poorest in the hemisphere, and we didn't need to do much more research. We believe that per capita GDP (PPP) is actually a better indicator of how a country is generally living. PPP stands for Purchasing Power Parity. One US dollar in Haiti buys more than in other countries, so Haiti residents are doing better than GDP without PPP would indicate. We believe the Haitian PPP per capita GDP of 2,900 USD is more accurate than the $1,800 per capita GDP because it better represents the standard of living. The PPP calculations conclude that although Haiti is extremely poor, the few dollars that they have goes a little further because prices are generally lower.

Human Development Index

The HDI assumes that education and life expectancy, along with GDP, is a better indicator of the human condition than just GDP. The HDI, like GDP, can improve on the aggregate as the majority of countries improve their human condition. The good news is even the poorest countries are doing better according to the Human Development Index. It isn't all good news for Haiti though. In 2021, Haiti ranked #163 in the HDI and dropped three positions in spite of the fact that their HDI number showed a slight improvement. This is because the three other countries that surpassed Haiti were improving at a faster rate. Without a government in place and with gangs taking control and rioting, I would fully expect Haiti to drop significantly in ranking as their HDI number will surely plummet. Although our Economic Mission currently drives only the financial aspects of HDI, we believe that as people leave hopeless poverty, they can eat better and have some degree of healthcare, which improves life expectancy. We also believe that more kids will attend school in a community that is served by an Economic Mission.

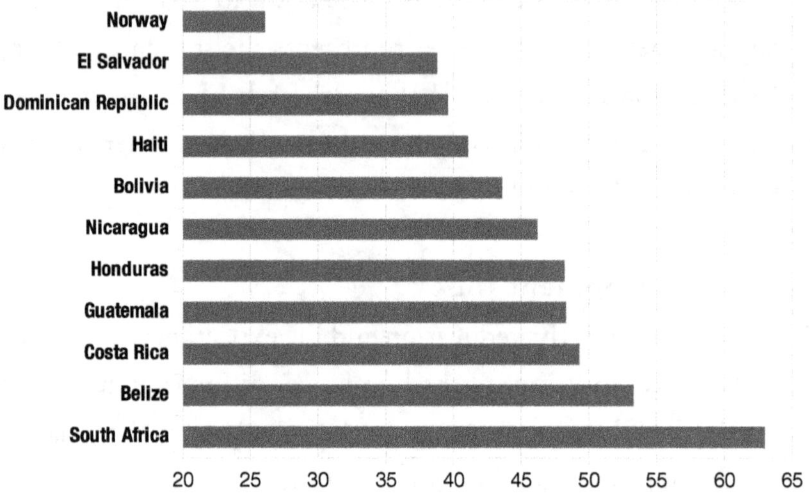

The Gini Index

The Gini index, or Gini coefficient, is an indicator of income equality. This is important because if there is a low per capita GDP and a high degree of income inequality, it can be expected that the poor are doing even worse than what the Per Capita GDP indicates. If the Gini index shows equality, then it can be assumed that the poorest third of that country might be doing better than what the Per Capita GDP indicates. Costa Rica, for example, has a high degree of income inequality and their GDP is relatively higher than other Caribbean countries. Costa Rica, in spite of the relative wealth, may have areas of hopelessly poor people and might be a good location for us. Logic could dictate that relatively wealthy countries with pockets of extreme poverty could be safer for Economic Missions because those countries will have more developed police forces and government resources.

The Social Progress Imperative

The Social Progress Index and other information that comes from the Social Progress Imperative (socialprogress.org) is helpful and interesting. Well… interesting for people who like plowing through charts and graphs. Using a wide array of data, they dig deeper to better portray an image of what life is like in individual countries. This dats is used by governments, businesses and NGOs. To someone who values statistical data, their annual index and the occasional email is highly valued. By using the raw data, users can take deeper dives in areas that go past GDP and HDI. The trending information is very useful, and users learn where potential countries are trending in a multitude of categories, like quality of diet, women's rights, improvements in sanitation, and about seventy-five other categories. By signing up for their emails, we get invitations to webinars and information on a variety of topics that could affect the Economic Mission. They quantify a wide variety of data into an index, but examining the columns for target countries provides an amazingly clear picture of that country.

Online Searches

This is a new option that we just added, and it provides outstanding results when it comes to security and understanding the political environment and volatility of the culture. By routinely googling "Belize today news," researchers can get a basic idea of the volatility of Belize. Poor countries with better security and infrastructure would be better for an Economic Mission as long as we were able to truly pull a community out of hopeless poverty by operating successfully. It is important to remember that the Economic Mission performs best in poor and densely populated areas, so less volatility may indicate that this country might be safer but not necessarily more comfortable. Looking back, because of Haiti's crooked government; setting up a company in Haiti took a lot of energy that could have been used to grow the company.

The Power of Prayer

After considering several locations, we then want to approach our decision with what Jesuit philosophers call indifference. Often indifference means not caring, but in this instance, it more closely means without bias. For example, I personally would want to operate in Belize long before Haiti, but am I able to do great work in Belize? That is what needs to be answered in an indifferent manner. Finally, I turn it over to God and the power of prayer.

Why Haiti? A Brief Case Study

Any objective review of economic information points out that Haiti is clearly the poorest place in the Western Hemisphere. Their per capita GDP hovers at $1,800, which is about 2.5% of the US per capita GDP. They are at the bottom of the HDI, and they will surely drop after reading what I am getting when I google "Haiti news today." On a positive note, the Gini coefficient rating shows that Haiti is ranked with the middle of the world. I believe this is because the Haitian economy is so small that there is a low ceiling for wealth. Haiti is a country that proves that no matter how bad life can seem, things can always get worse. All economic information paints a very grim picture of Haiti, and unfortunately, that picture is correct. Haiti with all of its poverty and other social issues means an Economic Mission can make a drastic change for good.

Selecting a Location for the Economic Mission

There is a simple guideline for selecting locations: If the location that is being considered is comfortable, it is not the right location for an Economic Mission. The best locations for Economic Missions are the world's worst places that are densely populated. If there is a nice restaurant with beautiful tables, it is not the right location. If the locals have cars, it is not the right location. If there is a consistent source of electricity and water, it is not the right location.

The more impoverished the community is, the greater the difference the Economic Mission will be able to make.

The goal for my Economic Mission is to lift as many people as possible above the UN's extreme poverty line. If most of the town is living above the extreme poverty line, the impact will be limited. When selecting a location for an Economic Mission, it is most important to remember the objective. Pulling a community out of poverty requires specific conditions, and there are a number of considerations. Depending on what the Economic Mission is manu-facturing, some of these considerations may fluctuate. We chose Praville, Haiti, and as we go through the conditions for loca-tion, I will explain how we felt Praville fit our conditions.

Three reasons we selected Praville.

1. Because most people in Praville were significantly poorer than average Haitians. When we visited, our eyes confirmed all of the economic information we had studied. It was obvious that Praville was hopelessly impoverished and the majority of the population was living below the World Bank's $2.15 extreme poverty standard.

2. Praville was densely populated. This meant employees didn't have to walk far to get to work and we were assured of having an adequate talent pool. That also meant that our payroll rippled quickly through the local community. We expect the multiplier effect to produce a stronger ripple in areas

that are densely populated. The ripple effect helped us reach critical mass and effectively pull more people out of poverty.

3. We had a support network through the Sisters of Saint Joseph of the Apparition, the bishop of the Diocese of Gonaives, and all of the friends of Rodney Merard. Getting things accomplished and managing finances were a reality because of my support network.

The one thing we should have given more consideration

We learned in Haiti that we should also consider community and government instability. Haiti is, was and always will be a political and impoverished mess. If we had set up in a different country, although we would have been less effective, our factory would be operating today. If we were in Belize or the Dominican Republic, our model wouldn't work as well, but unlike our Haitian factory, we believe our factory would be accomplishing its mission. We recognize that any area that needs an Economic Mission is inherently unstable, but there is a threshold where an Economic Mission's effectiveness is diminished due to instability. We wouldn't consider a mission in Iraq or Afghanistan and maybe we should have thought twice about Haiti.

4 Factors for an Economic Mission's Ideal Location

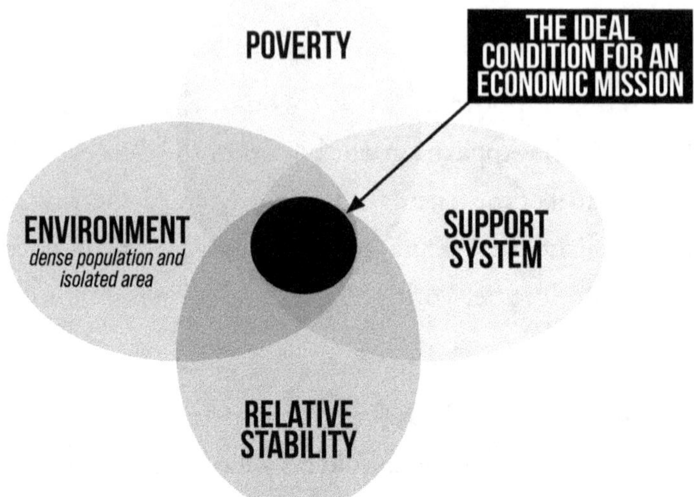

The optimal location for an Economic Mission can be determined at the intersection of these 4 ovals. If there is a local support network in a densely populated area of people who are living on $2.15 or less per day and there is a degree of governmental stability, an economic mission could be very successful.

Poorer Than Average Haitians

Third World countries don't have detailed or reliable economic research on individual villages. Instead, missionaries need to do their own research and arrive at their own conclusions. As we were searching, we found a location in Praville. Visually, it was easy to see that Praville was more impoverished than the surrounding Gonaives area. Residents lived in unfinished houses as squatters, and as I drove through the main street in Praville, I saw roadside shops but never saw anybody buying anything. The children were grossly underweight and clearly these children weren't eating every day. As I walked through the streets of Praville, I talked with people to define the poverty level. Very few people were making enough to provide the basic necessities for themselves or their children. Some were getting diaspora income from relatives in the US. My limited research was verified during job interviews, because one of the interview questions was "How much money are you currently making?" and after more than one hundred interviews, very few people were making more than $30 per month. `

An Amazing Support Network

> # REMEMBER
> *IF YOU DON'T HAVE A SUPPORT NETWORK,*
> *DON'T CONSIDER THAT LOCATION FOR*
> *YOUR ECONOMIC MISSION.*

I couldn't be at the factory on a daily basis, so I needed a support network. I am defining a support network as someone who can keep an eye on the mission and execute actions on a high level as needed on a consistent basis. A good support network will see themselves as part of the mission, and their loyalty goes beyond volunteering. My general manager was qualified, but having a support network can be a resource for him, and it is also good for him to know he is being watched. We had needs for services, local experts and craftsmen. Without phonebooks or websites, finding these people can be a challenge. A support network that sees themselves as part of the

Economic Mission is needed or there will be a constant battle to manage the simplest of details.

The Sisters of Saint Joseph of the Apparition were absolutely amazing. From the beginning, they shared my vision. They gave us a piece of land to build the factory, and they gave us everything they could so we could pull the community out of poverty. They are awesome because they do their work with a smile on their faces and the love of Christ in their hearts. The factory in Praville was a significant part of their lives. We strategized, debated and had candid conversations that moved the factory forward. They became a payment broker for me. I would wire money to their account, and my general manager would go to the nuns for payroll and to pay other expenses. The nuns would email my accountant a record of everything they spent, and our US bookkeeper could put it into our accounting program. They also made sure devotions at the factory happened daily, and they walked to the factory a couple times a day just to be sure everything was good. They helped me help the people around the factory, and they told me when I was doing something dumb. When I visited the factory, I lived in the convent.

As we began making plans to do an Economic Mission, I met Rodney Merard. Rodney became so committed and valuable to our mission that we named the bird on our Pravi Apparel logo and on the cover of this book after him. Rodney had friends in Gona-ives and Port-au-Prince, and these friends were always able to help. Rodney consistently handled the grind of details on a day-to-day basis without getting frustrated. He worked more closely with the government and their useless bureaucracy. It was with Rodney's help that we found people to help build our factory. One of Rodney's friends was a lawyer who was able to get stuff done for me. Rodney brought people in that could do miscellaneous things, and he discussed Haitian culture with me. He would accompany me on many visits to our Praville factory. I enjoyed his company and his perspective.

This was my support network as the factory opened. These people were dedicated missionaries who didn't see themselves as volunteers. They were integral in the process of getting the factory opened.

I was also fortunate to have a chance introduction with Andy Apaid which turned into a key relationship that helped me with engineering concerns, shipping to the US, and dealing with the Haitian government. He assigned an engineer, Gilbert Durand, who worked tirelessly on turning our factory into the efficient production facility that it became. Like the sisters, he was constantly putting me on the right path. I was glad I had them as partners because I enjoyed them as people, and they made my factory a competitive entity.

When opening a business in a part of the world that is unknown, having a network of people that are willing to support the mission is of paramount necessity. These three aforementioned examples show a level of commitment that is required by the support network. These people were attracted to the mission because they saw the opportunity and they believed the Economic Mission could pull an entire community out of hopeless poverty.

SIDE STORY

What I Learned By Living With Nuns

As Praville became more dangerous, it was safer for me to live at the convent that was next to the factory. It was very secure and convenient and the nuns thought they were funny calling me Sister Jim and telling me that I needed to wear a dress. While living in the convent, I realized that nuns have it way better than priests. Nuns easily avoid all of the politics, whereas priests constantly get caught up in parish politics and complaints. Further, nuns have only a fraction of the meetings that a parish priest has. In the Gospel of Luke, there is the amazing story of Martha and Mary. It seems to me like priests have the role of Martha while the nuns have the role of Mary. If I was going to live <u>with</u> them, I had to live <u>like</u> them. I might consider myself a good enough Catholic, but attending all of the daily Masses, evening prayer, morning prayer and late-night rosaries is how a superstar Catholic behaves. I had to "up my game" spiritually . It was a wonderful experience

Advantages of Dense Population

For purposes of location selection, densely populated means thousands of houses that are very close together. There are rarely second floors, and in poor communities, they are more like shacks. Most houses are detached, but they are only ten to thirty feet from other houses. Most urban locations have about three thousand to five thousand people per square mile. In Praville, the lot sizes are generally smaller and the typical house had seven or eight people living in it, so we felt like there were about 7,500 people living within the square mile that housed our factory. The government had no information, and we really didn't need to know exactly how many people were there.

This photo was taken from the 2nd floor fire exit of our factory. Praville had thousands of little houses like the one in the center of this photo. There is no running water and several houses would share a latrine. Most houses had between 6–11 people living in it.

A dense population has three main benefits:

Praville had street merchants who had the goods that employees would want to buy after they got paid. On payday and the Saturday after, each dollar bill that we gave on payday could be handed over multiple times in a single day before it left the one-mile circle that surrounded our factory. If $8,000 are circulating on the impoverished streets where people are hungry and need the basics, it is a logical assumption that payroll is being spent over and over again in quick succession. Simply put, if the hungry finally have money for food, it will be spent quickly. Because of its population, Praville was almost like its own micro-economy, so the payroll was spent over and over again in the area that was close to the factory. It is this quick spending and ensuing multiplier effect that helps us reach a critical mass when it comes to combating poverty in a community. We believe if the factory is in a rural setting, the payroll would scatter, and although it would help many people, reaching critical mass would require higher payroll dollars, and the transition of the dollars from hand to hand would be slower.

Like in the US, living close to work has advantages for employees. If the factory is in a rural setting, employees have long distances to traverse before they get to work. In a country with no public transportation, employees may need to walk one or two hours to get to work and another hour or two getting home. That could make an eight-hour workday a twelve-hour time commitment. An employee can only give one hundred percent, and if they are burning four hours and 750 calories on an effort to getting to and from work, that is depleting the one hundred percent that they can give to the factory. By having the factory close to employees' homes, they arrive at work safely and with more energy than if they had walked a long distance.

Further, a rural setting has fewer people, which means we would have a diminished pool of talent. A shallow talent pool could affect our efficiency and quality. As we opened up in Haiti, I realized that working on a sewing production line takes more skill, dexterity, and stamina than I originally thought. Like all businesses, talented staff drives success, and a limited talent pool would limit our success.

Keeping Our Distance

In Haiti, we made the conscious decision to stay away from Port-au-Prince and even Cap-Haitien, which is Haiti's second largest city. We had numerous concerns, but our biggest concern was the political powder keg that was in these cities. Further, prices and pay scales were generally higher in Port-au-Prince, which meant that we would be paying our people more, but they wouldn't be living better. I also felt that many company expenses would be higher in the cities. Too many factors could affect the prices or the quality of life for our employees. There were many days when strikes closed factories in Port-au-Prince, but we were working in Praville because we were away from the "noise."

Faith-Based Community

In Praville, there seemed to be a church, or more like a shed that was used as a church, on every corner. We were able to work with pastors of all congregations to extol the virtues of our factory. I felt that an abundance of local churches would provide a more subdued environment for my factory. It is why Karl Marx called churches "the opiate of the masses". It doesn't sound nice, but as a Christian, I believe there is truth to that. A benefit to having a culture of faith is that the community should also have higher moral standards and less violent temperaments. These virtuous standards should produce a better culture for our business to operate. I also felt great knowing that locals were praying for the success of our factory.

Trucking Friendly

Finally, and to a lesser degree, consider the ease by which trucks can get in and out of the factory facility. This would be a challenge we faced in Praville. The cost of trucking from Port-au-Prince was almost thirty percent of the cost of putting it on a container and shipping it from Miami via a boat. When we shipped equipment, we were always concerned that the computerized components were going to be damaged by the rough road. I still like Praville as the best location I could get, but I recognized the shipping and trucking headaches that would come with it.

When selecting a location for an Economic Mission, it is important to first find a country that is impoverished on a per capita GDP basis and on an HDI basis. If an Economic Mission is operating in a country that is relatively poor instead of hopelessly poor, their effectiveness will be limited. Further, demands for higher wages may come as employees see other people earning more, which may affect the mission's ability to compete in the global market. Although higher payroll is great, it is only great when it is pulling people out of poverty.

After a country is selected, it is important to get into the right situation by picking the best location possible. The mission can thrive if it has local oversight and is situated in the environment that best serves the goals. It is almost like picking a spouse because the factory will be paired with that location for a long time. Discuss the location ad nauseam to be sure to get it right.

"Character cannot be developed in ease and quiet. Only through experience of trial and suffering can the soul be strengthened, ambition inspired, and success achieved."
Helen Keller

"If a man is called to be a street sweeper, he should sweep streets even as Michelangelo painted or Beethoven composed music or Shakespeare wrote poetry. He should sweep streets so well that all the hosts of heaven and earth will pause to say here lived a great street sweeper who did his job well"

Martin Luther King

10 - HIRING EMPLOYEES

We paid fairly and as promised. Nobody else did.

For a common worker, the minimum wage is $5.60 per day. Nobody pays that, and most workers in Praville are earning $3 per day or less. Even the police get cheated. They are trying to keep law and order, and they are getting shot doing it. Although they make more than minimum wage, when payday comes around, they are routinely sent away empty-handed. My head of security is a policeman, and he didn't receive his full salary once in the summer and fall of 2022. This is not good when there is a wife and child depending on that income. It is not unusual for employees to work all week and get nothing or a fraction of what they were promised. Among Haitian workers, there generally isn't an expectation of prompt payment. If an employee leaves their job, they will never get paid for what they did, and finding another job will be challenging. The vast majority of employees I interviewed made less than $30 a month. This was the environment that existed when I began interviewing for employees at Grateful Inc. in Praville, Haiti. Naturally, we had plenty of people that wanted to work in our factory.

In my former position, I did plenty of hiring. When I didn't hire well, I also ended up firing. Nothing in my previous job experience prepared me for hiring for an Economic Mission. On hiring days, there were hundreds of people applying for thirty or forty jobs. Each person represented five to ten people back home that they wanted to feed. It was a very stressful time as interviews started at 7AM and went to 7PM without any breaks except for the bathroom. Each candidate had hope, and I knew by the numbers that many of these people would be rejected. I loved providing people with jobs, but I hated knowing that fourteen other people are getting rejected for every person I hire. I believed that by closing interviews, I would be giving the appearance that jobs were being bought or obtained using unscrupulous tactics. Several pastors recommended employees, and I later found out that these recommended employees were required to pay a fee to the pastors as long as they had the job. Sadly, I wasn't confident that the churches saw that money.

The hiring process needs to be managed from outside of the local organization. Every manager, employee, supplier, and even the nuns would recommend people for the job. The pressure to hire these recommended people was enormous. Most recommendations were for people coming from out of town or those that didn't fit our profile. The greatest amount of pressure inadvertently came from the nuns. I owed the Sisters of Saint Joseph of the Apparition enormously. When I was there, they fed me, gave me a place to stay and even let me use their car to get to the airport. They never asked for anything; however the nuns would send me very old people with no stamina or ability and asked me to hire them. I didn't like explaining to the nuns, or my employees, why I wasn't taking a recommended employee. I thought hiring would be a satisfying opportunity. In reality it was replete with disappointment and negative emotions.

In Praville, interviews are a once-in-a-lifetime opportunity. They told me what I wanted to hear and consistently lied to me to get the job. When candidates learned that we were asking about basic computer skills, everybody became a computer genius. When we told them that we were looking for people who could sew, everybody had a sewing machine in their house. Making it even better, everybody was already magically making polo shirts and uniforms. There aren't background checks or references because nobody has a working cell phone and most businesses don't survive. Occasionally I saw a diploma from a trade school. Hundreds of interviews meant hundreds upon hundreds of exaggerations and instances where people told me what I wanted to hear. On top of that, I didn't speak the language, and I was working through Rodney as my interpreter. That slowed the process down, but that also permitted me to focus on body language. I was able to tell when someone was exaggerating by their body language.

Interview candidates took their opportunity very seriously. Candidates came with handwritten resumes and dressed up to show me how important this job was to them. Some guys had secondhand tuxedo jackets that were purchased on the street. Some people brought their children and let me know that this job meant that their child would eat and survive. I felt like that was a little unfair, but I would've done it too if I were in that situation. They were responding to a very rare opportunity. The vast majority of candidates had never had an interview and were extremely nervous.

Blonncy, who ended up working in our cutting room, was first in his class in high school and college. He was friendly and polite, and when he saw the factory going up, he began to learn English so he could talk to me about getting hired. Without a doubt, Blonncy was my most ambitious interview in my entire professional career. Blonncy was out of college several years, and this was the first interview he could find. I loved these individuals too quickly, and having to reject them depressed me. I said no too often for my liking.

Most of the candidates had the drive and desire and could have been trained. They were good people who were doing what they needed to. After the hirings were announced, I knew not to be seen on the streets because the people who didn't get jobs wanted to have a word with me, and hopefully that was all they wanted. Because there were so many candidates that were awesome and motivated, my margin of error was actually far better than when interviewing in the US.

Criteria for Hiring

With so many interviews in one day, we were "cranking" up to six interviews an hour. We knew what our model employee was. When we saw that someone wasn't in our model, the interview was over. Dashing someone's hopes in 2 minutes was demeaning for them and bothered me. As interview days progressed, the questions we were asking got circulated, and people knew the responses we wanted. This made it harder to be sure we got our model employee.

People Are People

As soon as I arrived in Haiti, it seemed that everybody was telling me that Haitians were different. Initially, I bought into that but I soon realized that Haitians were just like everybody else. They had the same desires as I did. They wanted to take care of their families, find love and enjoy life. Haitians were people just like everybody else in the world. The environment in Haiti was brutal and Haitians were reacting to that. They were just trying to survive and they were doing what I would have done if I was in their shoes.

Because we had so many interviewees, we increased our standards beyond what we thought we needed. Our model employee was someone that had finished secondary school and passed the national test. Less than thirty percent of the people we interviewed met that standard. Post-secondary schooling or training, especially in tailoring, was a plus. We also needed people that would be able to work on a production line with stamina. Sewing ability wasn't the most important qualification, because we felt we could successfully train anyone with stamina and dexterity. Remembering our mission, they needed to be poor so they could be pulled out of poverty. We also wanted them to live close to the factory. We were trying to set up a micro-economy and pull the entire community out of poverty. It was hard saying no to a person that had traveled fifty miles for an interview, but we did it. We also wanted them to be living very close to the factory for security reasons. We felt that they would know if security threats were coming, and they did warn us about the attack on our factory. Attitude was important. We believed that a great work culture was possible and very important; therefore we looked for people with personality and smiles. We weren't there to convert anybody, but as a Christian mission, we wanted Christians working for the organization. We would then empower them to evangelize and do the work of the mission throughout the community. After the interview, all candidates were tested for dexterity to be sure they were able to do the work.

We needed to find the best people so we could be competitive. It was important to not get drawn in by sad personal stories. I didn't want to be callous, but everybody had hungry children and was living in poverty. Almost every interview had a story and everybody needed this job desperately. It was difficult for us to not get drawn into personal situations, because ending poverty was the mission. We needed to remember that we had to stay competitive in the worldwide market so our company could grow. We had to hire the best talent we could get. We had the Vacated Expenses Advantage, and it was important that we didn't squander that opportunity by hiring with our hearts instead of our heads. We are not an NGO. This could not turn into a competition where the people that were in most need got the job. We needed to put together a great team. We are a business, and we need that team to win. In hiring and in many other situations, I found it difficult to have my head in sync with my heart. I had to deliberately remind myself of what we had to do.

What About Eyeglasses?

As we were opening the factory, we began the very arduous process of hiring our initial staff. As described in this chapter, training was inconvenient because they had to live in Port-au-Prince and the conditions in which they lived were horrible. It was their best opportunity even though they didn't fully trust me. As my initial staff began training, I was told by the training organization that 13 of my people needed to be removed from training because of poor eyesight. They were not able to thread needles or accurately read a measuring tape. In fact, the training facility already dismissed them and they were going home on the next bus. My comment was, can't we get them glasses, to which they responded that they didn't have money for glasses. For $430, all 13 had eye exams and got glasses. From that point forward, I had the trust of the whole staff.

Understanding the Local Laws and Cultures

On our first round of hiring, I didn't have a comprehensive understanding of the Haitian culture when it came to work, nor did we understand all of the regulations. In the first year, we were constantly surprised by rules and laws that changed everything. Instead of an employee manual, everything was spelled out in a contract. There were rules for severance pay, and they had twice as many vacation days as in the US The most disturbing rule was that every December, every employee got paid a "thirteenth month." In essence, we were paying the December salary twice. This was bad because we were already paying as much as we could because we remembered that payroll in an Economic Mission is an output. An extra $32,000 in December gave our employees a good feeling, but if it were provided throughout the year, it would have provided a better prosperity.

Employee Training

Our first employees had a brutal training program. Each Sunday at 2PM they left their families and went to the USAID training facility in Port-au-Prince. They lived in poor conditions, and they were ninety miles from their family, which is difficult when they traditionally spend most of their life within a mile of their house. It was a difficult time, but we didn't have options. The training program was great, and when the factory opened, it was only a matter of weeks until we were producing high-quality shirts. During that time, employees were meticulously doing their jobs, and production levels were low. As they got familiar with their jobs, production levels increased.

Like everything in Haiti, USAID went in a different direction, and the training facility was closed. The discounted rate we were promised for training evaporated. When the training center closed, we were able to hire their best trainers and open our own training facility in our factory. We treated the people that went through the difficulties in Port-au-Prince as heroes because they made life better for everybody who followed them. As our second and third waves of employees were being trained, they could earn money doing miscellaneous jobs from time to time. The 2nd and 3rd wave of trainees didn't have to leave their hometown either. The trainees knew the employees and understood the company culture through osmosis. It was just a better situation for the trainee and the company.

About Management

Hiring managers in an uneducated, Third World country is difficult. A Third World secondary education doesn't prepare students to compete in the world market. Further, the concept of creative thinking and leadership by example is unheard of. Most of the managers and supervisors see success as getting the job, not working. In other words, once they have the job, they can stop trying so hard. Managers in Third World factories have never heard of Kaizen, 6 Sigma, or any other quality or production improvement strategies. The cumulative result of these deficiencies results in an inability to execute. In order to compete in the world market, companies need to be able to get the job done in a changing market. Companies need to execute better through creative thinking. At the same time, companies need to be committed to delivering consistent results.

We coveted managers that were passionate about the mission of pulling people out of poverty. They knew that we needed to be competitive in the world market in order to provide the number of jobs we desired. They also knew that the Economic Mission model is something new and that they could make a difference in their world for their friends. They wanted to be heroes. This made the difference, and our managers became more aggressive in achieving goals. In essence, we wanted to "psych up" our managers to such a degree that they would do whatever they needed to succeed. It worked because what we are doing was heroic and even patriotic on some level. We were bringing that part of Haiti back to a former greatness. It was about pulling people out of poverty and providing opportunity. This is far more motivating than squeezing an extra two percent on the bottom line for a faceless financial group in Los Angeles. In the end, culture and mission are amazing tools that drive businesses forward.

Third World Management Training

Management training came down to oversimplified summaries of business principles. This was highly effective because managers understood clearly what they needed to do to perform on a higher level. Concepts from the book Good to Great, Management by Objectives, and strategy became paragraphs that were talked about in training sessions. I learned that we probably over-complicate training concepts in the US. Maybe keeping it simple and having passionate people is a better way. Our management team had the difficult task of getting inexperienced employees to work together and make polo shirts that could compete in the world market.

The training that served us best came from Ryan Holiday's book on Stoic philosophy titled, The Obstacle Is the Way. The book stressed that by overcoming the obstacle, companies can find the path to growth, profitability, opportunity, and even greatness. Our Economic Mission had plenty of obstacles and numerous big obstacles. I simplified it further by saying, "The only reason Nike sells more shirts than us is that they have had more time and have cleared more obstacles." Before long, our managers were having obstacle meetings where they were selecting what the obstacles were and how they were getting past them. Our attitude towards problems changed. Production was climbing, and we were maintaining quality. When our factory was invaded and destroyed, several of our managers saw the attack as an obstacle. They were right, and to move forward we will need to get past this disaster. This is far more than I thought I could expect from a one-page book summary of a book.

We also introduced the concept of Kaizen. We had an engineer who understood Kaizen, and it is simple enough to implement. Basically, Kaizen means continued improvement. Kaizen improvements start on the production line and work their way to top management. It is a process where a company makes a commitment to improve a little each day. It isn't a cerebral concept, but with consistent application and corporate commitment, it should make huge differences. Our management could never get the production line people to participate, and that was because of the Haitian culture that lacked creative thinking. I believe our management could have been more creative and gotten better results from our production people. From time to time, when positive things happened, management would point to Kaizen, but we've never managed to bring this into the heart and soul of our business. Our people want to be great, but the concept of every head in the game has never developed. By effectively implementing Kaizen, we could have done better.

Both managers and production employees saw the Economic Mission as an once-in-a-lifetime opportunity, and they did everything they could to maximize results. That was beautiful.

"**Money won't create success,
the freedom to make it will**"
Nelson Mandela

11- Managing Employees

*Surprisingly, managing employees from thousands
of miles away isn't as difficult as it may appear.*

At our factory in Praville, we hired awesome people who do their best to make a quality polo shirt at a great price. I credit this in part to the hiring process. Managing employees gets less difficult when the company starts by hiring great people. Unlike the US, employees in Praville realize that there is no safety net and that they need to succeed, and that made all the difference. In the US, if someone fails at their job, they simply redo their resume and start looking. In Praville, Haiti, if the factory fails, employees will never make this much money again and their time of unpaid unemployment will be measured in years. The lack of opportunity drastically increased the level of commitment because if there is failure, there is no other job out there. Because of our people and their absolute need for success, we are competitive. Managing employees is about maintaining their commitment and keeping standards high. We did this on an emotional level, and we have policies in place to keep it this way. Workplace culture was enormously important. When employees understood the mission and that the success of the mission is on their shoulders, success was almost guaranteed. All employees understood that this is something that has never been done and that they can be heroes by being successful. They knew their success would help lift their starving neighbors out of poverty. That was motivating.

Managing employees takes more than motivation. It isn't about getting more out of employees as much as helping employees to be their best selves. Our employees have lived a life of starvation and pain but I can't diminish my expectations because of that. The temptation to coddle them is a very slippery slope. If we demand less, we will get less and we will need to pay less which will do less good. Truth is, we all responded positively to the challenge and winning on a daily basis gave life meaning. For me, it became about helping them maximize their opportunity. It is about helping them to pull themselves out of poverty and letting their determination do the rest.

I have a deep respect for our employees. They are committed and passionate. In spite of a deplorable education system, violence, hunger and infrastructure, they show up with smiles on their faces and they did a great job. Sometimes I questioned their thinking, but I never had a reason to question their heart. They wanted to be great and everybody bought in. They aren't creative thinkers and it is difficult to get the production line people to offer suggestions. Shortly after we began operations, I had confidence that this team could compete in the world market. I was pleasantly surprised how quickly production ramped up.

Here are some of the things that we did to help our employees be awesome.

Never Be an NGO

Although NGOs are necessary, the NGO mindset is the enemy of the Economic Mission way of thinking. NGOs are for helpless people. They generously come in like angels and help people that can't help themselves. The Economic Mission is about empowering people so they don't need help. It is about independence. Until now, almost none of our employees had any long period of time where they were independent. When things go wrong and employees struggle, the addictive embrace of an NGO is naturally tempting. Independence doesn't always feel like a wonderful gift, but it is better than the alternative. Employees will want it easy when they get tired or when times get tough. The Economic Mission needs to be sure to remind employees that they were called to greatness and something better. They know what winning feels like and that has the power to pull employees through difficult times.

Incentivize

People respond to positive stimuli. As a sales manager, I always said managing salespeople was easy. Put the incentives in the direction that the salespeople should go, and they will surely go there. We wanted everybody to be on time so we could get a fast, productive start each day. The added "On Time bonus" worked beautifully. If they punched in on time and didn't punch out until after quitting time they received an extra $2.50 every day. If they forgot to punch in, they also lost the bonus. Because of that, our employees were on time over 99.5% of the time and they always punched in. With eighty employees using their fingerprints to clock in, we would have four hundred opportunities for employees to be late each week. We usually had one or two late punch ins per week and they lost their On Time bonus.

SIDE STORY

The Missed Bonus

I bragged constantly about the remarkable 99% plus on time percentages we achieved. We achieve this in part because I "stacked the deck". Before we started operations, we deducted $2.50 from the daily amount that we were budgeting for each employee and then we added it back as a $2.50 On Time bonus. It is important to remember that many of these people were living on $2.15 or less before they began employment. It was a big deal. One morning, as Haiti was sliding into disarray, one of our employees was 7 minutes late because there was gunfire on her street. Making her case stronger, she crawled out of a window and walked well out of her way to avoid the gunfire. When she got to work, she asked if she could still get her bonus. If there ever was an excuse that was worth consideration, that was it. According to our general manager, other employees were interested because if we gave her the bonus that would open up the "excuse flood gates." He said it felt like everybody was looking to see what we would do. Ultimately, we ended up not paying her the bonus because we knew it would bring more excuses in the future.

From the perspective of our employees, they were literally making tons of shirts worth ridiculous amounts of cash. We needed to be sure they didn't become complacent. Incentives were paid for performance over budget. In other words, when we were paying production incentives, our labor cost per shirt was well below our goal. Once employees arrived, the company culture kicked in and they were productive. We offered production bonuses because we felt it was responsible to pay our employees for being efficient. It worked because attendance was over 99% and production ramped up more quickly than we expected. We also offered bonuses for reaching all-time-high production figures, and that became celebratory because they got extra money and were recognized for excellence. Incentives were great because it allowed us to make payroll larger which is what was pulling the community out of poverty. The incentives also generated higher production levels which made incentives affordable. It was another way for the employees to win and when the employees won, the company also won.

Be Process Driven

Employees are most efficient when they know exactly what they are to do in all instances. Our production engineer was very good at putting the processes in place so each employee knew what to do when things went according to plan. They also knew what to do when things didn't go as planned. When employees know exactly what to do, they are far more efficient. That's the power of process. It is important to see processes as evolving and to constantly keep improving. This continued improvement is the essence of Kaizen. Continued improvement was our challenge and we wanted to continually improve at the pace we wanted. As demands for polo shirts got crazy, we fought to prevent a slide in quality. We saw a quality drop that came with a demand for high production and that was because our processes were not as developed as they needed to be. That could be expected because we were in our first year of production with inexperienced employees and ownership. We were operating under strenuous conditions and cracks began to show. The terrorist attack will give us an opportunity to start back up with better process.

Be Willing to Discipline and Fire

There is an ugly trait in human nature and in any job setting. People look to see how far the rules can be stretched. If leaving early was permitted, then eventually, everybody would leave early. That is human nature. If we accepted inferior performances, we could expect other people to slip in their efforts as well. We get what we expect, and if we expect less, that lack of expectation will infect the entire organization. We optimistically expected high quality and efficiency and the employees basically delivered. We needed to be an organization of excellence. An Economic Mission thrives on commitment and excellence, and when we aren't getting that, we need to discipline. It was very rare that we saw a defect from someone who just didn't care. Our employees cared immensely and that made the difference.

Preach Debt Avoidance

It happens in the US, and it happens in Haiti. As people get a steady income, they begin to believe that they can live better by jumping into debt. Debt is nothing more than future money that can't be spent. Without looking down the road, they sell their financial freedom. Just like in America, they buy things they don't need with money they don't have to impress people they don't know. It is similar to America in the 1980s when it was cool to have a credit card and people used them foolishly. (We still do!) In both instances, naïve consumers who can't delay gratification sell their financial peace of mind. Life could revert back for our employees if they got in debt.

Training included more than sewing skills. Employees learned how to stay safe, personal health and even earthquake/tsunami safety. We considered devotions as being a special kind of training because we were helping to develop the whole person. As Praville's new high earners, it was also important to train them on personal finance and debt avoidance.

The temptation was even greater for our employees in Haiti because having debt is seen as a Haitian status symbol. In Haiti, interest rates are often above 25% which further handcuffs employees. It is important to have the ownership and general manager constantly promoting savvy and frugal financial habits. In presentations to employees, I would often make indebtedness seem foolish and for people who couldn't control themselves. I would tell them if they wanted more money to spend in the future, they needed to stay out of debt today. Employee indebtedness has one other ugly side effect that damages the effects of our Economic Mission. As payroll is used to pay debt, it isn't being used to pull people out of poverty. Dollars used to pay debts never hit the street where it could do good things over and over again.

In an Economic Mission, employees work like their lives depend on it. An Economic Mission is naturally set up for great employees to come to work every day and do a great job so they can pull their community out of poverty. By selling the mission to employees, and having the policies to help keep employees on the path to success, they were able to change their lives.

This is a photo of our fabric room. To an employee in Praville, this is job security. It proved to them that we had orders and they had job security. It was always a good day when a shipping container of fabric arrived at the factory.

12 - STAYING SAFE

*Security is about doing the right things so
you and your stuff remain safe.*

"Blan banm lajann" is what I heard most often when I was on the streets in Haiti. If we are driving somewhere, I constantly hear people scream, "Blan banm lajann," at the car. "Blan banm lajann" is heard wherever I go. "Blan banm lajann" means "white man give me money." To the majority of people in Praville, I was a walking piggy bank with endless amounts of money. Wealth and poverty are relative terms. I am the poorest guy in the room when I am my friend's guest at the fancy country club, but when I am in Haiti, I am pretty sure I am the richest guy in town. Even though I rarely carry cash, I am very rich compared to the people that surround my Economic Mission. To their neighbors who are impoverished, my employees are rich on paydays because they have $80 in their pockets.

It's a Security Risk.

The police are untrained and unmotivated because they usually go unpaid. Many police officers see missionaries and foreigners as a walking money tree, and they will also take what isn't theirs. When I am in Haiti, I am in a country that the US State Department put at the top level of their "do not travel" list. They cited kidnapping, robbery, and other violent crimes. It was perceived that I had money, and almost everybody wanted it. The majority of Haitians wouldn't take what isn't theirs; however, there are many people that would do whatever they needed to get my money. Instead of going hungry, a successful kidnapping could feed kidnappers and their families for several years. I don't know who they are, but I know there are people in Praville who would kill me for $50. These are realities, and this is why I need security for myself.

Traveling and Staying Safe

Security to this extreme degree was new to me. In my former life, I ran a cashless business and had very few assets that were worth stealing. We knew that internal theft was a possibility, and clients not paying their bills felt like theft to me. I also felt robbed when our account executives over-tipped waitresses because they were cute. That was the extent of my vulnerability, and therefore I was very trusting and even naïve. "Blan banm lajann" wasn't always said politely. Hearing "Blan banm lajann" all the time put me on notice. I had to learn how to operate in a secure manner, and I needed to learn it fast.

When doing business in Third World countries, security is a major concern, and building a security network and strategy is of paramount importance. It could save a missionary's life or prevent a kidnapping. I worked with a consultant who had experience in foreign security operations, and his experience gave me confidence. I am never comfortable, and my guard is never down. Staying safe requires deliberate preparation, and having a security consultant in the US and another consultant near the Economic Mission is imperative. As Haiti went from bad to total lawlessness, I saw enough to make me paranoid. That paranoia has kept me from being robbed, kidnapped, or murdered. We felt the biggest threat to me in the ninety-mile journey from the airport to the factory was kidnapping. Of course, robbery comes with kidnapping, so we were preparing for the worst. My consultant told me a few things that surprised me and a few things that were easily comprehended. Online research is not enough, and the best security requires strategy, not a check off list that was printed from a travel website.

Here are some security protocols to ponder:

→ I wanted to be nice, so I blamed all of these protocols on my security consultant. I would say that if he found out that I didn't follow protocols and I got kidnapped, he wasn't going to help because I didn't help myself.

→ Never completely trust any security personnel. The majority of kidnapping victims are delivered up by people the victim knows. The lure of $500 is irresistible to many security guards in Third World countries.

→ Be paranoid because foreigners and missionaries are never truly safe. Bad things happen when these people let their guard down.

→ When someone is inflexible about a change in plans or becomes adamant about staying on schedule, there is cause for heightened concern. Is it a set up? Is there additional reason for concern in this situation?

→ Drivers, like security guards, are even better at delivering up kidnap victims. I only knew details about three kidnappings, and in all instances, the driver drove off the route and into the arms of their kidnappers. This risk is best minimized when potential kidnapping targets are doing the driving. Caution is suggested for taxi drivers, Uber drivers, and even government employees.

→ Never ever stop the car. Some kidnappings occur when a van pulls across the road. If the car can't go around, then simply spin the van out of the way by hitting it at the back tire, and keep moving. If the only escape is to drive through a grocery store, then driving through a grocery store is what must be done.

→ There are tracking programs for phones and computers. Buy several programs for each device and have a person back home who knows how to access these devices. Amazon has recording devices, tracking devices, and tiny cameras. I purchased them all because staying safe was serious business.

→ It is extremely difficult to "trail a car" when the car periodically doubles back. This is a good habit to establish.

→ When being picked up at the airport, I would get photos of cars, license plates, government IDs, and the people who are on the security detail. I also take a video of the surroundings.

It is important to email or Dropbox the photos and videos to someone who is out of the country before departure.

→ Do everything to know the security climate of the country. Generally, the US State Department does an excellent job informing citizens of dangerous places. I would also register with the State Department, and then I would receive updates as areas became dangerous.

→ As a potential kidnapping target, I made sure that I picked the bathroom where we were stopping because the driver can take me into a robbery situation by saying that he needs to use the restroom. My traveling partners were all male, so we stopped on the side of the road and only when I indicated we should. It was faster, nobody was around, and it was just safer.

→ Never accept a suggestion when someone proposes an alternate route, a faster route, or stopping at a specific place, because this could result in a robbery or kidnapping situation. It is best to eliminate the possibility of a bad situation by never stopping.

→ Strive for time and place unpredictability. Travel different routes whenever possible. Never leave at the time, or even on the day that is on the itinerary. Keep the itinerary on a need-to-know basis, and have false appointments on the itinerary. It is important to be as unpredictable as possible.

→ Although I conscientiously objected from the armed services in college, I carried a gun while I was in Haiti. The whole idea is to not use it. It isn't like TV. If I killed another human being, it would affect me for the rest of my life. Living with a gun, especially in a situation where there is an elevated risk of having to use it, is not cool. It didn't make me a tough guy, and it was not good for my morale.

→ I would keep an eye on drivers and security people who were using their phone for texting. I was at a disadvantage here because I didn't know the language. I would ask my local security manager to check texts every once in a while to be sure nothing that would elevate my risks was being sent.

Time and Place Unpredictability

It is routine that makes kidnapping or robbery easy. For that reason, I never left when I said I was going to. We would leave at unexpected times. There was only one plane from New York each day, and that meant my arrival time was predictable. We had to make allowances for that predictable occurrence. Sometimes we would catch lunch at the safe hotel that was across the street from the airport, and that lunch could take two hours. When I had to do business and visit government offices, I would drive whenever possible. I was able to use Google Maps, and I always took different routes. I was particularly nervous when I left the bank because there were always people out front watching me. I always took several security guards, and they were never the same two guards twice. Being unpredictable is critical for safe arrivals.

Kidnapping Protocol

Paying ransoms provides an enormous incentive to kidnappers. We had a firm kidnapping protocol in place. My biggest fear was that if my employees or I got kidnapped and we paid ransoms, we would have rewarded kidnapping behavior. After that, we could expect somebody to get kidnapped on a weekly basis. The Catholic Church paid ransoms, and priests, nuns, and schoolteachers were getting kidnapped nonstop. Our policy was succinct and clear. We would never pay a ransom no matter what and no matter whom. This ransom protocol included me. I would have paid a ransom for my wife, so she could no longer be able to go to the factory. Further, in the event of a kidnapping of one of my employees, we would pay rewards for the capture of these criminals, and we would promote these rewards. We always had money that was accessible in the US so we could operate in the event of a kidnapping. It is the paying of ransoms that fuels the kidnapping culture that Haiti currently has.

The Best Way I Traveled Safely

As an Economic Missionary, I am doing God's will, and staying safe is part of that. When I got in a car, even if I knew the driver and security team, I wanted to be sure they knew that offering me up came with serious risks. I made sure they knew I had a gun. I told the driver I would shoot him if he turned off course or if he stopped in the event of a potential kidnapping. Eventually, I was driving myself with my driver sitting in the backseat. To me, it was a matter of controlling all of the factors that I can control.

I had a challenge to prevent a planned kidnapping where my security would give me up. I understood that unfaithful security staff would get paid by kidnappers to simply not act in a kidnapping situation. To address this, I also told my security people that if someone with a gun stepped into the street trying to stop us, they should shoot immediately because I was shooting immediately. Surely the person in the street would be shooting back, and we wanted to kill them before they killed us. In my mind, I was true to what I was saying. I wanted to be sure that they knew they also had a lot to lose if they were setting me up for kidnapping.

This may sound abrasive and harsh, but there were over 225 kidnappings in Haiti in the first ninety days of 2022. Missionaries and white Americans are favorite targets. I am both, and I haven't been kidnapped. My paranoid actions might have made the difference.

Staying Safe at the Destination

Comfort is secondary, and security is primary. I was very fortunate. When I was in Haiti, I slept in a convent that was behind twelve-foot walls and locked up like a prison cell from the inside. There were bars on the windows and the balconies, and no access was available from the roof. I was glad it was a brick building because in the event of a fire, I wasn't getting out. Further, my security, which did not have the keys to the convent, was next door at the factory and reachable by radio.

My Potential Kidnapping

One afternoon we had a meeting with a Haitian bishop and we had to travel to his house. As per standard protocol, I took my gun. As we were leaving, it was suggested that bringing a gun was disrespectful and I should leave it. I thanked him for his suggestion but told him I was taking the gun. He became argumentative which made me even more concerned. Then he suggested that he wouldn't go. At that point, I felt the chances were very good that I was being set up. I forced him to go and a couple minutes later, he was texting. I concluded that there was a good chance that I was being set up for a kidnapping. Within two weeks, he was fired for theft. It was a lesson that I could easily be a statistic and I needed to remain paranoid.

When I had to stay at a hotel, security was the only concern. One hotel in Port-au-Prince was secure, and I stayed there exclusively even though I paid too much and didn't really like the experience. When traveling with my security team, I would switch rooms with my security. I was in their room, and two or three guys with guns were in my room. We never left the hotel or convent grounds if we didn't absolutely need to, and when we did, it was never at the time that was stated. I love martinis, but when I was staying at a strange hotel, alcohol was off limits, and I never drank anything that I didn't open except for the coffee and juice that was on the breakfast buffet. In Third World countries, there is no reason to go out. There aren't good entertainment options and Haitian restaurants leave a lot to be desired. We found a hotel north of Praville that we used when I made trips to the north. They were the safest option. They served spaghetti noodles with ketchup and cut-up hot dogs, so that is what I ate, in spite of the fact that there was a restaurant two hundred yards away from the front gate.

I never forgot that in relative terms, I was incredibly rich when I was in Third World countries. Further, never forget that a portion of the population of that country will do whatever they can to get money. Travelers and missionaries can't be too safe nor can they be too paranoid.

It is important to point out that Haiti is in such decline that nothing short of explosives and automated weapons could have slowed the terroristic destruction that occurred in our factory. As of this writing, people with money can't buy food because there isn't any food to buy. For me, it is easy to empathize with the people who pillaged the factory. Gangs have all of the food. If a local was not in a gang, he and his family were going hungry. Further, if they are not in a gang, locals are in danger of being killed and having their children raped or murdered. If you were a parent and your children were home dying from hunger, wouldn't you raid a warehouse? I would, even if it meant risking my life. Every business that had food, or might have had food has been raided. Desperate people do desperate things, and rich Americans are the people to target.

The question is, even after order is restored in Haiti, how long will it be until the gang mentality leaves this generation. I can't find a statistic, but there may be 100,000 people or more who were once good people who have turned to violence. It is hard to fathom a country, about the size of Maryland, where 100,000 thieves, murderers, kidnappers and rapists are freely roaming the streets. It would be naïve to think that when a government is put in place, these thugs will revert back to their former and better versions of themselves. From a security perspective, it is very difficult for me to hold out any hope for Haiti to return to a civilization in the next 20 or 30 years.

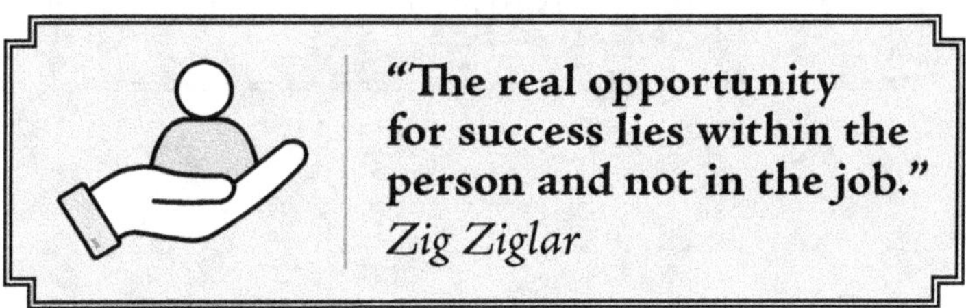

"The real opportunity for success lies within the person and not in the job."
Zig Ziglar

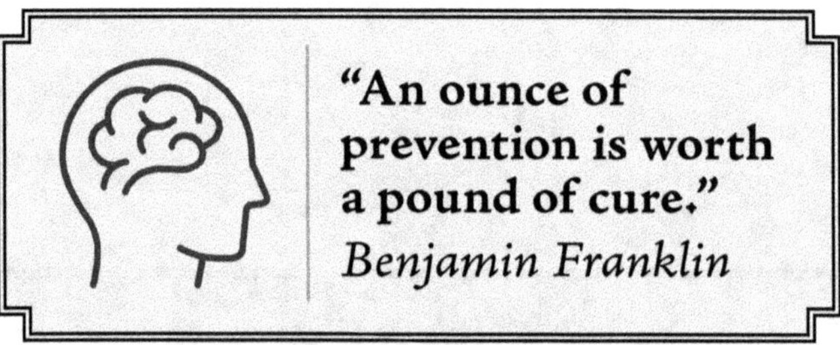

"An ounce of
prevention is worth
a pound of cure."
Benjamin Franklin

13 - AVOIDING FINANCIAL FRAUD & THEFT

Relaxed financial security protocols will become very expensive.

When foreigners understand that they are seen as a walking piggy bank by the majority of people that surround the Economic Mission, they will continue to add layers of security. Financial theft is a direct approach. If it can be done, embezzling is the easiest and cleanest way to steal. Kidnappers don't want the headache of kidnapping. They just want the money kidnapping gets them. Nobody wants to break in and steal a computer or a machine then find a market to sell it. They just want the money they can get from selling the computer. Finding a sneaky way to embezzle is the easiest and cleanest way for a thief to get money, and therefore it is also the most attractive. Somehow, embezzling on a routine basis doesn't seem as bad when it in fact does far more damage than the one-time theft of a piece of equipment. If an embezzler can steal something every week, they can massively improve their lifestyle. To someone who is extremely poor and violently desperate, White Americans are perceived as abundantly wealthy. Stealing from a filthy rich White American is viewed as a victimless crime. Sure, in an objective sense they are stealing but lines get blurred for people who are living a life of violent desperation. I get it.

Smart Economic Missionaries will understand that this will be the most favored form of theft and will continually make enhancements and adjustments to their security based on this reality. I believe that nobody who worked in my factory would do me bodily harm for $500. I also believe there is a significant percentage of my employees who wouldn't have a problem embezzling $500 from the White American who owns the big factory. As caring people, we naturally grow to like the people in the Economic Mission. Liking employees can turn into trust, and every betrayal seems to begin with trust. I was once told by a wise businessman that," If I felt like I was being cheated via embezzlement; I should consider that maybe I am". If that isn't the case, the extra caution will help keep company assets safe. A little bit of paranoia is almost required when theft is a legitimate or likely risk.

I learned early in my professional career that controls won't make embezzlers honest, but good systems and controls will keep honest people from embezzling. Further, it is irresponsible for an Economic Missionary to allow financial temptations to sit in front of Third World people. It is important to have controls securing company finances. There are a number of online recommendations that can be easily implemented. As with other security practices, checking the boxes helps, but adequately protecting company interests involves a deliberate effort. Having a working knowledge of the inventory, payroll, and accounting systems will help when implementing controls. As with all other security protocols, it is very important to continually improve controls.

I routinely try to role-play myself as an employee in my Economic Mission in different capacities. As a role-playing employee, I try to find ways that I could embezzle from my company. I tried to see what I would do if I wanted to steal from the Economic Mission and uncovered ways and have put additional controls in place when possible. I remain cognizant of those vulnerabilities, and I want to limit and control them. I owe it to my employees to eliminate the temptation of theft. Although I may have lost a little fabric to a line employee, it is my management that can steal the most. I can't give the exact details at this time because I would be tempting my employees should they read this part of the book. Most of the time, I would be thousands of miles away from the factory, and that will also provide opportunities for theft. The financial controls need to account for that.

It Is Your Fault

I recognize that I am working with some of the poorest people in the world who are coming out of extreme poverty. If I allow financial theft temptations, one day soon I am going to be a victim of financial theft. I believe that it is my fault if I didn't do everything I could do to prevent it. The employees that pulled off the manufacturing miracle are good people but I would be fooling myself if I thought these people never stole to get what they needed. I need to have empathy for the horrid situation that they came out of and the habits that were accrued while they were living in that situation. If I am not doing everything I can to prevent internal theft and embezzlement, then I deserve to be ripped off. It is my job as the factory owner to do everything in my power to keep my employees honest. It is important for employees to know that I am paranoid about theft. I need to constantly enhance my systems to keep employees honest.

The Nun Fund

Earlier in this book, we highlighted how a support network is extremely important. We didn't have a petty cash fund. I mentioned the Sisters of Saint Joseph as integral to our operation. They were kind enough to manage my finances locally, and we set up an account called the Nun Fund. When an employee needed money for something like payroll or supplies to pay for a service, they would request that payment, and I would approve it. Sister Margaret would then provide the funds but only after it was approved. We then had a very simple Excel file ledger, and she would meticulously put all expenses in that ledger. My accountant used that ledger to produce our financial statements. Every expenditure is cross-referenced on my email and WhatsApp account. Without the Nun Fund, I would be giving too much control to my general manager, therefore tempting him to embezzle. As previously stated, it is both naïve and immoral for me to create temptations on my part. As airtight as this seems, it doesn't keep employees from getting kickbacks for overpaying for products, and there are details in payroll that might be overlooked. It is the responsibility of the Economic Mission to eliminate temptations, so we must find a way to place controls on the aforementioned items.

No Second Chances

I tell my managers that there are no second chances when it comes to theft. When someone has embezzled the first time, they surely knew it was wrong. They have proven their lack of self-discipline. When an embezzler is given a second chance, the owner that provided the second chance has communicated that they are either naïve or gullible. The message that is sent to other employees in the company is that everyone can embezzle until they get caught, and then they get a second and maybe even a third chance. I once caught an employee who was keeping the change from transactions. When confronted, he explained it away as a mistake, and although I didn't believe him, I gave him a second chance. I basically told him that it was okay. Several months later, I caught him stealing from the employee payroll fund. Looking back, I deserved what I got, and that was my fault. Besides having weak controls, I basically told my employee that it was okay to steal.

Centralized US Accounting

We believe that by doing fewer transactions at the Economic Mission, we can decrease the amount of temptation and opportunities for theft. For that reason, all of our accounting, billing, and check-writing functions are done out of the United States office. I see my bookkeeper on a daily basis, and I have a copy of our books on my computer. I sign every check. Each of these functions diminishes the temptation that sits before our US bookkeeper. We still have to continue the process of removing temptations wherever we can because good controls keep honest people honest.

In summary, from their perspective, I am filthy rich, and they are not. Employee theft and fraud are the cleanest and most preferred ways to steal, and employees can even convince themselves that it is a victimless crime. Without adequate controls and by allowing temptation, internal theft will happen.

"Trust but Verify."
Ronald Reagan

14 - THE MODEL, MOMENTUM & FUTURE

Focus on the mission, and it will guide you.

By focusing on the goals of the Economic Mission, you will be guided as to how you should be operating. By starting each task with the end in mind, doing the right thing to benefit the mission becomes 2nd nature. Clearly the Economic Mission model is all about growing the factory in an effort to maximize the impact of payroll, which will pull the surrounding community out of hopeless poverty. It is far easier to keep a happy customer than to solicit new business. However, there are two concepts in this book that stand out and define the Economic Mission model.

Summary of Goals

1. Our first goal is to pull entire communities out of hopeless poverty, not just employees, and accomplishing that goal means maximizing payroll while remaining profitable.

2. The second goal is that in order to grow, the mission must be competitive based on price and quality and must successfully compete in the world marketplace.

These two concepts were often mentioned in the business plan and, after 18 months of production, they seem to be as important as ever. Yet when I was meeting with my friend and consultant, Paul Armstrong, he asked me a question that changed everything. His question was, "If you want to employ as many people as possible and put as much payroll on the streets as you can, why wouldn't you sell as many of these large contracts as possible?" I can't believe I didn't see that earlier. We were focusing so much on our floundering small scale sales efforts that we didn't pursue our greatest opportunities. We never expected to land both a multinational fast food franchise and a Fortune 500 company in our first year. Combined, these two contracts could be for 150,000 shirts or more each year. If we could duplicate that sales effort, plus enhance our US sales effort, we could have four or five production lines.

The Exclusive Factory

Why do we need to dictate what we are selling? What if we solicited loans from Angel Investors and purchased factories that would exclusively operate on a contract basis for very large US-based customers? We could have an exclusive factory that worked only for one major customer. Can an Economic Mission get on the same side as our customer that needs hundreds of thousands of shirts and pants? The job of the Economic Mission would be to generate savings and make our large, US-based company more money. We would produce the products that they need exactly like they need them to be. Our employees would make their products like their lives depended on it because they do. We would get a very affordable payback on the equipment. Our employees would be incentivized and would over deliver. The company that is receiving the product from the Exclusive Factory understands that we are trying to pull communities out of poverty and that maximizing payroll is a major corporate goal. These companies could market these products based on their commitment to ending poverty in this community. Best of all, these companies would benefit from a stable source of manufacturing. We have approached one company with this model, and I remain optimistic.

The exclusive factory offers great benefits.

→ We are closer than China, so we could respond more quickly. If we carried a base inventory of materials, our factory could make products in days and get it to the US in only weeks. Companies wouldn't have to overstock and could manage variations in demand more easily. The challenge would be to remember that little piggies get fed, while hogs get slaughtered. Greed is not good.

→ Because of our Vacated Business Expense model, we can compete with any company in the world. Who makes all of the uniforms for McDonald's? Who makes the Adidas and Nike polo shirts? Do we need to stick with polo shirts? Who makes pants for the US retailers? The value proposition doesn't lie in the polo shirts. Our value proposition lies in our business model.

Could we build factories for very large companies so we could exclusively produce what they need almost as quickly as they need it? If so, we could more aggressively pull entire communities out of poverty by generating very robust payrolls.

Improving Our Current Model: Vertical Integration

As tragic as the terrorist events that closed our factory in Haiti were, there will be amazing opportunities when we build elsewhere. It takes at least six months from order date to receive fabric in the Caribbean. Using solution-dyed yarns, we will be able to weave and knit fabrics overnight that can be turned into shirts for customers the next day. We believe three different denier yarns could produce a wide array of fabric choices that would make almost any customer happy. Instead of a warehouse of fabric, we would have a warehouse of solution-dyed yarns in all of the colors that we offer. We could make almost any fabric in an array of weights, colors, or anything else they need with these yarns. This would be an enormous competitive advantage for our factory.

The new location would also afford us the opportunity to perform in-line embroidery services. The services would allow us to embroider shirts for companies, colleges, and sports teams at a faster pace. Further, large Division I colleges could keep their offerings more flexible and order smaller quantities of more animated patterns and colors without the risk of getting stuck with large quantities. The turnaround time would be superior.

We would learn from the tragedies in Haiti and probably not have an enormous factory but instead two or three smaller factories that would appear less ostentatious. We would also implement better neighborhood engagement practices. Most importantly, we would be in an excellent position to pull hopelessly impoverished communities out of poverty through robust payrolls.

In the US, we would continue the effort to gain sizable contracts to keep our factory busy. We would implement different strategies for smaller orders and we would probably entertain a partnership. If we could remove the costs associated with the sales call, those sales would be profitable, and those profits could be reinvested in new technologies and the new factories.

Haiti Production

Going back to the factory where we were is highly unlikely. First, it is common knowledge that this factory can be invaded and everything removed from it. Further, it would take an enormous investment to bring the factory back to an operational level. So much was learned about manufacturing polo shirts that if we went with a larger factory, it would be in a different layout. I don't want to turn my back on the wonderful employees who developed the Economic Mission concept with me. If it wasn't for this group, this Economic Mission model would only be theoretical. My hope would be to add micro-shops only to the extent that we were employing the people that were employed during the attack.

I am also committed to getting as many workers as I can out of Haiti. As I am negotiating factories with new countries, I will also negotiate work visas so I can bring people with me. It would be unreasonable for me to assume that I could bring everybody because that would diminish the purpose of the factory in the community where we are moving. Given the opportunity, I owe it to my employees to do something special.

The Big Challenges

There are two main challenges. First, we need to simultaneously increase demand as we increase output. Unfortunately, training workers is a slow process, so we must be proactive. The second challenge would be to raise money to build these factories. As an Economic Mission, we are not interested in donations. We would rather have Angel Investors with a promise of a payback on a zero-interest loan. As an Economic Mission, we would rather not take the stance of a begging 501(c)(3) charity. Instead, we want to partner with businesspeople to combat poverty one community at a time.

With everything that we have learned, the future is amazingly bright, and I am highly encouraged.

What Now

It is God's will and I have a burning desire to continue to develop the Economic Mission model. I have the experience and knowledge to pull thousands of people out of extreme poverty. With the help of God, I have the key to ending extreme poverty for countless people. I am obligated to use my Economic Mission model to combat world poverty. I have seen the horrors of poverty and I have seen what an Economic Mission can do in a community. I profoundly desire to make this my life's work!

I need to find Angel Investors and companies who can purchase our products. I need to find smart people who can ensure our production capabilities are everything they can be. I also need to find smart people who can generate business in the US. I need to keep inviting people to be part of something that is very special.

I need my Economic Mission model to be easily replicated so other caring people can use my Economic Mission model to free people from poverty. I need to learn from past mistakes and build on past triumphs.

I want to be a difference maker. For 20 years or more, I have known that the purpose of my life was to "MAKE A DIFFERENCE WITH LOVE AND JOY". Building Economic Missions will make a difference beyond my wildest imagination. I need to be sure I do that with love and joy. My calling is to build Economic Missions. It is the will of God and I choose to joyfully submit to that.

Simply put, God didn't bring me this far just to bring me this far.

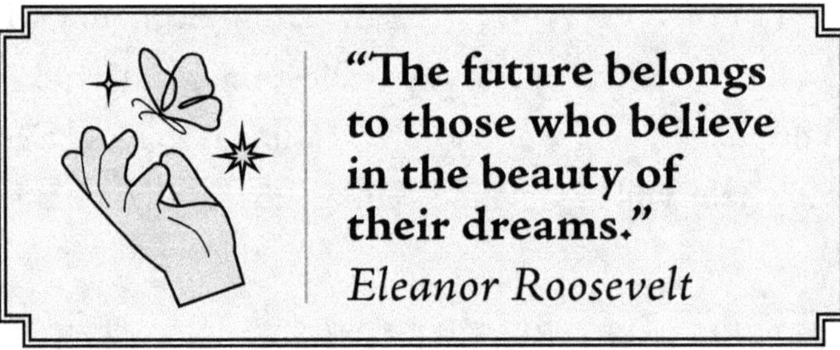

"The future belongs to those who believe in the beauty of their dreams."
Eleanor Roosevelt

15- WOW!!! What an amazing ride...

I have had some amazing things happen and this has been a remarkable journey. I have been developing the Economic Mission concept for over 4 years and I almost missed the amazing journey that I was on. It was only when I started to dictate the steps of my journey back to me that I truly appreciated it... I am thankful to God, my wife, friends, my small group at church, family, business associates and even strangers for helping me see how awesome my journey is.

There are Positives

The terrorist attack on the factory is not a good thing, but attack has afforded us opportunities and lessons that will help us move in a better direction. We have accepted the suffering that comes with the attack and with that acceptance comes opportunity. Here are a few ways without deep detail.

→ Keep Me Humble – As God was making miracles happen and as we were landing major accounts, it was difficult to stay humble. Pride is as deadly for a business as it is for our souls. I was doing something great and I knew it. The destruction gives me an opportunity to recognize that this is God's project and I need to always remember that. For that, I am reluctantly thankful.

→ Improve the Concept – With the daily demands of keeping the factory operating, we didn't have adequate time to dig deep and discuss all of the obstacles that were threats to our highest degree of success. With the factory closed, we have time to address more obstacles and the next version of our factory can be better and even more competitive. We made mistakes when we opened our first factory and we have a great opportunity to do something truly exceptional with our next factory. Romans 8 says "We know that all things work for good for those who love God, who are called according to his purpose" and we are empowered by this because we have purpose by the truckload!

→ Adjust the Sales Model – The small order sales model was broken. When we reopen, we will fix all of that and get it right so we can be strong into the future. We will also be more aggressive with our large account sales. We will forecast production and sales in a better way. We will sell tons of shirts to lots of big companies in the future. We can create bigger paydays that will provide more opportunity for more villages.

→ Add Systems – We were missing systems that would make life easier for both the US and Foreign operations. The attack and restart will give us opportunities to implement better systems and processes that will reduce mistakes and build efficiencies.

Losing Millions and Winning Championships

Everyone wants to know, so here it is… Jennifer and I personally lost about $2.5 Million in the terrorist attack on our factory. I was very shocked at what happened the next day. Nothing. Nothing happened. I am not extremely rich so obviously, losing $2.5 million affected my future plans for a better home and an ocean worthy catamaran, but I don't need that stuff. It turns out that the money didn't have a grip on me. The next day, the sun came up, Jen was there, the cat wanted fed and I had things to do. Sure this changes my plans, but that doesn't make my life any worse. Epictetus said, "Wealth consists not in having great possessions, but in having few wants." I am on an amazing ride that started years ago and did not end when our factory was destroyed.

It's what psychologists call The Arrival Fallacy except for me it was in reverse. It happens to professional hockey players after they win the Stanley Cup. These competitors say that winning is the greatest feeling and how this victory completes their life. Then they wake up the next day and feel in their hearts that nothing really changed. In essence, these players have worked their whole lives to achieve a goal and when they have arrived, they don't attain the thrill that they thought it would be. They are still sons and dads and they still need to work out because next season is around the corner. Losing $2.5 million and having the world around me get destroyed was my personal "Disaster Fallacy" factory. Nothing really changed and by living in the present moment, I realized that this destruction wasn't as bad as I feared. Albeit, I would rather have my $2.5 million back but I learned a lot about myself.

The Final Analysis

The big question regarding my role as an economic missionary seems to be, "If you could do it all over again, would you?" The answer to that is a resounding yes! I have never worked harder, nor have I ever lost more money. However, that is outweighed by my understanding that while many people fight the symptoms of poverty; I am in a unique position to cure extreme poverty. Making a difference is what drives me and fills me with immense satisfaction. Through the grace of God, I made an enormous impact on thousands of people in Praville, Haiti. The job, the people, and the challenges brought out the best in me.

Now, I find myself in a position to replicate that success on a long-term basis, and I am inspired by the transformative changes I witnessed in Praville. I also believe that God is calling me to continue this path. Although retirement or returning to the comfortable advertising world may be tempting, those options pale in comparison to the fulfillment I experienced in Praville. Very few people in this world hold the keys to truly free people from poverty and I am fortunate to be one of them.

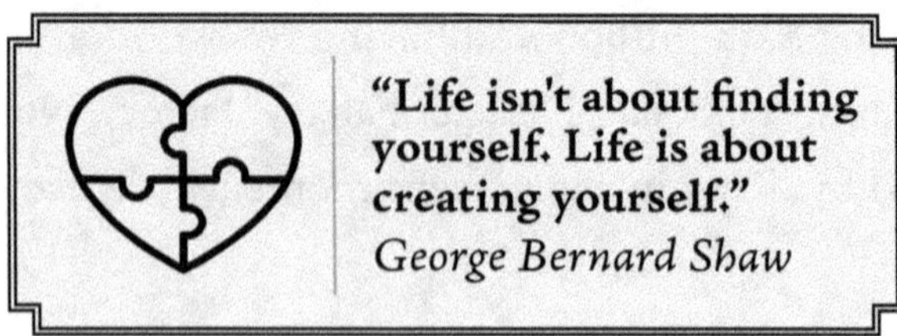

www.ingramcontent.com/pod-product-compliance
Lightning Source LLC
Chambersburg PA
CBHW050907260726
48660CB00001B/72